CW00866288

Bedtime Meditation Stories for Kids

A Collection of Short Meditation Tales to Help Your Children and Toddler Fall Asleep Fast, Learn Mindfulness and Thrive.

By Sarah Puppet

Table of Contents

Chapter One: Scary Dragon Cliffs Spindles Ton

Close your eyes and be very still, taking a big deep breath in through your nose and slowly and gently breathe out through your mouth. Take another deep breath in and slowly and gently breathe out through your mouth. One more time, big deep breath in and slowly and gently breathe out through your mouth and relax, feeling peaceful and calm. Once upon a time, there lived a king in Bamboo Castle. He had a beautiful wife and two children. The son's name was Child Wind, and his daughter Margaret. So, Child Wind set off to look for happiness, and soon after his departure, the Queen Mother died. The king long and bitterly cried for her, but once during a hunt, he met a beautiful lady and loved her so much that he decided to marry her. And he sent home the news that he would soon bring a new queen to Bamboo Castle. Princess Margaret was not happy to find out that someone would take her mother's place. But she did not murmur, and on the orders of her father went out on the day of his arrival at the castle gates to meet her stepmother and give her all the keys.

Soon the wedding train appeared. The new Queen approached Princess Margaret, who bowed low to her and held out the keys to the castle. Having zipped and looked down, the princess said:

"Welcome, dear father, to your chambers! Welcome, my new mother? All that is here is all yours!" - And again, she held out the keys to the Queen. One knight from the new Queen's procession exclaimed in admiration:

"Really, there is nobody in the world more beautiful than this northern princess!" Then a new queen broke out and spoke aloud:

"It would not be bad for you to add: "except for the new queen!"

Then she muttered in an undertone: "Her beauty will soon disappear..."

That very night the Queen—and she was the famous sorceress crept into the dungeon and began to conjure. Three times, she cast a spell; nine times, she created a magic sign and enchanted Princess Margaret. Here is her spell:

"You will now become a terrible dragon, and you won't be saved - so I command! And if your brother, royal son, you won't get three kisses forever remains a scary dragon, and you won't be saved - so I command!"

So, Lady Margaret went to bed, a beautiful girl, and woke up a terrible dragon. In the morning, the maids entered to dress her and saw a disgusting monster on the bed curled up in a circle.

The dragon reached out and crawled towards them, but they screamed away. And the monster wriggled and crawled, crawled and wriggled, until it reached Spindleston Rock. It wrapped itself around the rock and lay there, warming its terrible face in the sun. Soon, all the surrounding residents involuntarily learned about the terrible dragon of the Spindleston rock. Hunger forced the dragon to crawl out of the cave and devour everything that came in its way. And then, people finally went to the powerful Wizard and asked him what to do. The Wizard consulted with his assistant, looked into the magic books, and announced:

"The scary dragon is Princess Margaret! The dragon is tormented by hunger, so he devours everything in his path. Take seven cows for him, and every day at sunset, carry all the milk from them to Spindleston Rock—all to the drop! And he will no longer touch you. If you want the scary dragon to turn into Princess Margaret again, and the Queen, who bewitched her, be punished according to her deserts, call from the sea the princess's brother – Child Wind."

So, they did. The dragon was fed milk from seven cows, and he did not touch anyone else. When the news of the sister's bitter fate came to Child Wind, he solemnly vowed to release her and take revenge on the cruel stepmother, and thirty-three Child Wind knights swore with him. They set to work and built a longship, and its keel was made of mountain ash. When everything was ready, they took up the oars and sailed straight to Bamboo Castle. Before they could see the corner tower of the castle, the Queen learned with the help of witchcraft that they were plotting something against her.

7

She called all her close demons and said:

"Child wind is sailing. So, let him not get to land! Raise a storm or smash his ship! Do what you want, stop him from landing on the beach! And the demons hastened to meet Child Wind. But as they saw that the keel of the ship was mountain ash," they retreated, powerless.

So, they returned to the Sorceress Queen, and at first, she could not think of anything. Then she ordered her warriors to fight with Child Wind if he landed near the castle and forced the terrible dragon to guard the harbor entrance. When the Child Wind ship appeared in the distance, the dragon rushed into the sea, twisted around the ship, and threw it off the coast. Three times he ordered Child Wind to row his people stronger and not lose heart, but each time a terrible dragon drove the ship from the coast. Then Child Wind ordered to bypass, and the Sorceress Queen decided that he despaired and swam away. But Child Wind circled the cape and calmly moored ashore in Bald Bay. He and his knights with drawn swords and bowed dashes rushed to smash the terrible dragon, which prevented them from landing on the shore. But the moment Child Wind set foot on the ground, the power of the Sorceress Queen over the terrible dragon ended. And the Queen returned to her chambers alone, neither demons nor warriors could help her anymore, and she knew that the hour had struck her.

When Child Wind approached the terrible dragon, he did not try to devour him. Child Wind had already brought his sword over the dragon, when suddenly from the terrible jaws of the monster, the voice of his sister Margaret was heard:

"Leave your sword and bow tight do not be afraid of the dragon! And thrice to my scales, touch your lips." Child Wind froze with a sword in his hand. He did not know what to think. And the terrible dragon said again:

"Leave your sword, bow to me and kiss three times! Hurry until the day is dead and cast a spell!"

And then Child Wind went up to the terrible dragon and kissed him. But the dragon, as it was, remains the dragon. Child Wind kissed him again, but

8

again nothing happened to the dragon. Then Child Wind kissed the monster for the third time. And then the terrible dragon with a hiss and roar recoiled back, and his sister Margaret appeared before Child Wind. Child Wind wrapped his sister in his cloak and hurried with her to the castle.

He went to the corner tower, climbed into the Sorceress Queen's chambers, and touched her with a sprig of mountain ash. Before he could do this, the witch cringed, wrinkled, and turned into a huge, ugly toad with wildly bulging eyes. The toad croaked, hissed, and jumped from step to step down the stairs. From that day on, Child Wind began to rule the kingdom instead of his father, and they all healed happily. And near the corner tower of Bamboo Castle and now there is still a vile toad. This is all she, the evil Sorceress Queen. In the end, take a deep breath in through your nose and slowly and gently breathe out through your mouth. Again, deep breath in and gradually and breathe out one last time, deep breath in and slowly and gently breathe out. Whatever you are ready, wiggle your fingers, wriggle your toes, give a big stretch, and slowly and gently open your eyes. But remember, shine as bright as you can always.

Chapter Two: Matchmaking for the Lizard Princesses

Close your eyes and be very still, taking a big deep breath in through your nose and slowly and gently breathe out through your mouth. Take another deep breath in and slowly and gently breathe out through your mouth. One more time, big deep breath in and slowly and gently breathe out through your mouth and relax, feeling peaceful and calm. Close your eyes and be very still, taking a big deep breath in through your nose and slowly and gently breathe out through your mouth. Take another deep breath in and slowly and gently breathe out through your mouth. One more time, big deep breath in and slowly and gently breathe out through your mouth and relax, feeling peaceful and calm. In the old days, the king of lizards lived with two beautiful daughters, and only one king's father knew how to call them. It was time to marry the daughters, and then the king announced that he would give the daughters to someone who would give them their names and give each son-in-law a bag of money. There was no end to the grooms! All the men in the neighborhood wanted to get the king's daughter and a bag of money also, but no one could guess the name of at least one of the girls. And Pavian decided to cheat. For three days, he, hiding, watched what the royal daughters were doing. And on the fourth day, Pavian bought two mangoes. Very ripe and beautiful.

Taking them with him, Pavian climbed one of the trees under which the royal daughters used to play. Pavian waited a long time, but one of the sisters went away somewhere. Then Baboon threw down the mango. The girl who remained under the tree began to call her sister to share the fruit with her. She began to call her sister by name. So Pavian found out the name of one of the royal daughters. The Baboon was patient and waited for his second sister to leave. Again, he threw down the mango, and the girl who remained under the tree also began to call her sister to share her find. She called her by name, and so Baboon recognized the name of her second sister. In those days, a stringent rule was established in the kingdom of lizards: "no one was allowed to speak with the king himself. If anyone wanted to talk with the king, he expressed his business to the king's chief adviser, nicknamed the Old Lizard, and he transferred everything to the king."

The day after Pavian found out the names of the royal daughters, he went to the palace. It was full of lizards. The Baboon told the Old Lizard that he wanted to marry the king's daughters, and the Old Lizard passed this to the king.

"Let him say my daughter's name!" — commanded the king. The Baboon named the Old Lizard, and he repeated them to the king.

"Here I will give you both my daughters and two bags of money in addition," the king announced.

"Take my daughters as a wife, Old Lizard, because you named them." The Baboon was very angry. He waited for the night and, under cover of darkness, stole a giant rooster that belonged to the king. The Baboon killed the rooster, ate it, and then went to the Old Lizard's dwelling and threw the bones and feathers of the royal rooster there.

"But that is not all!" Muttered Pavian menacingly. He heated palm juice almost to a boil and brought it to the Old Lizard.

"Drink the juice, it is so tasty," Pavian said insinuatingly. The old Lizard foolishly swallowed the juice and burned his throat. After this, Baboon offered hot sauce to the servant of the Old Raptor.

"Have a drink of sweet juice," said Pavian, and the unsuspecting servant drank and burned his throat too. The next morning the king was informed that one of his best roosters had disappeared. The king ordered all his subjects to be summoned to the palace.

"Where is my rooster?" The king asked.

"The Old Lizard has stolen it!" Cried the Baboon out loud.

"Bones and feathers wallow in his dwelling."

"So, you stole my rooster?" The king of the Old Lizard asked menacingly. And he cannot answer, he burned his throat with hot palm juice so much, he only nods his head.

"Is it true that the Old Lizard has stolen my rooster?" The king asks the servant of the Old Lizard. And he also nods, after all, he also burned his throat with hot palm juice, so much so that he cannot utter a word. Then the king said to all those gathered in the palace:

"Let the Old Lizard and name the names of my daughters, but he stole a rooster from me."

Therefore, I will not give him my daughters as a wife, and I will not give him two bags of money. So, it turned out that the Old Lizard and Baboon did not marry any of the royal daughters and did not receive a single bag of money. In the end, take a deep breath in through your nose and slowly and gently breathe out through your mouth. Again, deep breath in and gradually and breathe out one last time, deep breath in and slowly and gently breathe out. Whatever you are ready, wiggle your fingers, wriggle your toes, give a big stretch, and slowly and gently open your eyes. But remember, shine as bright as you can always.

Chapter Three: Beautiful Princess and the Unicorn

Close your eyes and be very still, taking a big deep breath in through your nose and slowly and gently breathe out through your mouth. Take another deep breath in and slowly and gently breathe out through your mouth. One more time, big deep breath in and slowly and gently breathe out through your mouth and relax, feeling peaceful and calm. Once upon a time, there was a beautiful princess whose heart was pure and full of love. His eyes were the same color as the sky when it was clear. Her hair, wavy and golden, fell on her back like tender caresses. Her sweetness was unique; she loved any person or animal; even the flowers whispered her name gently in the wind. Every petal that fell, every single plant, beautiful or straightforward, shed a tear for it and expressed a desire: that the flower can live forever without experiencing pain or losing its beauty. One day, a unicorn passed over the earth, silent as the air peered into people's hearts. But of all those people, he was struck by only one, a beautiful princess, with a heart so pure that it pushed her to cry for a petal fallen from a flower.

Her beauty and heart were so pure and fascinating that she was enchanted by it. Every day, the unicorn went to observe the princess, who he considered a rare pearl without imperfections or impurities. The admiration he felt towards him became very strong, like an enveloping and relentless fire that he could not keep hidden. So, on a full moon night, he decided to go to her, where the sky and the sea became one. That same night, the girl who was locked up inside her room, heard a slight and subtle melody from a music box. The music, affectionate but sad at the same time, seemed to be played by the moon. It was so beautiful that the princess could not help but go out on the terrace of her magnificent castle to hear those sweet notes. But as soon as she got out of the window, she found something much more fascinating there. There before her eyes was a candid unicorn which seemed to come out of a storybook that they told her as a child. He looked her straight in the eye, almost as if he wanted to speak.

At this sight, the girl lit her face and had the same splendor as a newborn star. The wings of the unicorn were transparent, like clear air, but in the moon's light, they shone as they were in the view of a trail of falling stars. On the back of his back, he had placed a music box, the same from which that beautiful melody came. The princess fell in love with that magical creature from the moment their eyes met. But alas, their love was not possible, since the lifespan of a human being is very fragile, but their feelings were so strong, that they pushed them to escape this sad reality. The years passed; the princess slowly aged. And soon, he died. The unicorn was very sad and angry. Although too late, he realized the fragile life of human beings.

One day, he took the lifeless body of his beloved maiden from the bed in which he lay, and carried her to the shore of the beach as the sunset, with its calm and elegance, the sky was painted pink, and the face of the princess he brightened, like the first time she smiled at him. The unicorn made a promise to her before the full moon appeared in the sky: that her pure soul could shine forever. So, he absorbed his whole body into the full moon. And the unicorn let the seawater absorb himself. The princess, since she became part of the moon, could now shine forever. And the unicorn, since it became part of the sea, could admire and reflect all its beauty forever. Take a deep breath in through your nose and slowly and gently breathe out through your mouth. Again, deep breath in and gradually and breathe out one last time, deep breath in and slowly and gently breathe out. Whatever you are ready, wiggle your fingers, wriggle your toes, give a big stretch, and slowly open your eyes. But remember, shine as bright as you can always.

Chapter Four: Rich Girl and Dragon

Close your eyes and be very still, taking a big deep breath in through your nose and slowly and gently breathe out through your mouth. Take another deep breath in and slowly and gently breathe out through your mouth. One more time, big deep breath in and slowly and gently breathe out through your mouth and relax, feeling peaceful and calm. Once upon a time, there lived a rich pan, and he had one and only coloring daughter. Grooms come to her from all over the world to marry, but the finicky beauty says one thing:

"I'll go for the one who comes dressed in pure gold!"

And then a carriage rushed once, harnessed with six horses, a stately fellow came out of it, dressed from head to toe in gold. The beautiful woman gave him a pen in a hurry with the wedding. They began to prepare for the wedding, twelve tailors' day and night for the bride to sew a wedding dress, and for the groom, a wedding shirt with gold lace. On the wedding day, carriages ride one another more beautifully. They are distinguished guests, in the latter, a worthy groom himself. They married the bride and groom; the fun and dancing went on until you drop. Sweat pours from the bride in a stream.

A beggar on crutches hobbled to the wedding. They want to feed him in the kitchen, but he doesn't go to the kitchen, sat on the doorstep, and began to take a closer look at the guests. Here the bride and groom went dancing, suddenly the beggar threw up his hands, but when he shouted:

"Take a look, good people, take a look! Something I do not like about the guests! You have to look, and some have horse hooves instead of legs. Others have goose paws!"

The young husband heard his words, grabbed his wife in an armful, and ran into the yard, the guests hurriedly rushed into the carriages, whistled whips, and all rushed off! Here they are already outside the village. Suddenly, out of nowhere, a black rooster! The rooster screamed at the top of his lungs, and in the blink of an eye, the whole wedding fell through the ground, and in that place, the lake spilled. The young husband picked up his wife, rose to the sky, and flew away, nowhere. He was not at all a good fellow, but a dragon with twelve heads, with twelve tails! And to deceive people, he tied himself with straw plaits, and everyone was ready to swear that he was wearing pure gold, and he was kind and handsome.

Parents cry day and night that their only daughter has disappeared, and neither the rumor of her nor her spirit has completely withered, emanated from woe, wandering about like shadows. Once, a woman appeared to them, saw their tears, and began to ask why they were crying.

"But don't you know that we have the only daughter missing. If only I could find out, at least see where she is, what's wrong with her, she's right or ill!" - Wails the mother.

"Don't cry," the woman consoles her.

"Tears of sorrow will not help. I will help you find out where your daughter is and whether she is well or ill. I have a son, and he sees everything in the world, he will find her, wherever she is. I will send it to you today."

"Ah, send it, but only as soon as possible!" - Asked the mother. "How long is short, and that woman's son is already right there!"

"Is that you, Vivid?" - The father of the girl asked him.

"Me," the guy answered. – "Say what I have to see to find out!"

"Tell us where our daughter is and what she does?" Then Vivid looked around and said:

"Oh, sir, your daughter's unenviable life! After all, her dragon carried away. He hid your daughter among bare rocks in a dark cave. And she must scratch his twelve heads day and night so that he would sleep sweetly."

"How can I get her out of there?"

"Let us, if my brothers and I take up the matter. Where my middle brother hits with a pickaxe, a triple, insurmountable wall immediately rises, and my younger brother, over a hundred miles, is not just a mosquito, but also someone who is shot with a smaller shot."

"Get down to business, and I will give everything that I have, everything you want."

"Deal!" - Agreed Vivid. Mother gathered her sons on the road, gave everyone a full bag of bread, a bag of feta cheese, and escorted. And Vivid already knows where to keep the path and what is happening in the dragon's cave. They go straight, do not turn anywhere. They came and Vivid immediately rushed into the cave. He sees: the girl sits, scratch the dragon's head, the dragon slumbers, and holds it with its tails. I saw the girl of Vivid, got scared, and whispered:

"How dare you come to us? After all, a fly will not fly here either!"

"This is not the time to talk," he replied.

"You scratch your head so that the dragon doesn't wake up, but I know what to do. She scratches, and well done frees her from tails. Will remove one tail - the dragon will ask: "Wife, why does this smell like a man?" And his wife reassures him:

"You dream about it; you know that you can't get here either." He freed her from all twelve tails, and she followed Vivid quietly out of the cave. The brothers surrounded the girl from all sides and walked away. Then the dragon woke up, and after them, and she cried out in fear:

"Oh, don't give me away, oh, don't give me away!" Vivid said to that brother who has a pickaxe:

"Hit the ground with an eyelet, put down a wall," she screamed very loudly!

"No, it's too early, let it fly closer." And the girl screams all over, afraid that the dragon will grab her and carry her back. But only the dragon extended its paws to it, the middle brother hit the ground with a pickaxe on the ground, and the triple, tall wall immediately grew. The dragon ran around the wall and growled:

"Give me mine, and it's not yours!" And the girl cried out:

"Don't give me away! Aw, don't give me back!"

Tired of the brothers in this mess, they answered the dragon:

"There isn't yours here! Where lost, look there!" But the dragon rested and not from a place:

"I'll be idle until the end of the world, if you do not fulfill my desire, give me at least one hair to look at!"

"How are we going to give you a peek into the hair?"

"You have a pick, so make a click in the wall!" Shouted the dragon to them.

"Do not listen to him; do not show him anything!" - Vivid said to the brothers, and he knows that the case will end badly. But those were so tired of screams and cries of listening to what they agreed:

"What a little! Let him look!" He got his dragon. They showed him a hair, and he wrapped it around his finger and pulled the whole girl by the nose! All she could do was scream!

"Don't give me away!" The brothers see from under the very nose of their dragon drags the girl.

Then the marksman smiled: his turn came to distinguish himself and get the girl.

"The dragon will still dance when my time strikes!" And he began to wait. And the dragon is already far, far, almost invisible, with a mosquito, it has become a size.

"What are you delaying? Shoot!" - The brothers are noisy.

"It's not time yet," marksman.

"How not to be late!" - shouted Vivid.

"He's already with half a car!" Then the shooter aimed and time! He shot the dragon all twelve heads and twelve tails! The liberated girl rushed towards the brothers, the brothers to her. They took her to her father and mother, that was a great joy! Still would! After all, they had one-disconnected! The girl stopped waiting for the groom in discharged gold, right in her husband and the youngest of three brothers, marksman. And the other two are not in the loser: each received a rich reward and began to manage on his land. And then they found beautiful brides and played three weddings at once, and they were so funny, they didn't remember them either before or after. In the end, take a deep breath in through your nose and slowly and gently breathe out through your mouth. Again, deep breath in and gradually and breathe out one last time, deep breath in and slowly and gently breathe out. Whatever you are ready, wiggle your fingers, wriggle your toes, give a big stretch, and slowly and gently open your eyes. But remember, shine as bright as you can always.

Chapter Five: White Deer

Close your eyes and be very still, taking a big deep breath in through your nose and slowly and gently breathe out through your mouth. Take another deep breath in and slowly and gently breathe out through your mouth. One more time, big deep breath in and slowly and gently breathe out through your mouth and relax, feeling peaceful and calm. Once upon a time, there lived a king with a queen. They had a beautiful kingdom, and they happily ruled over them. Only one afflicted them, they had no children. Once, while walking through the forest, the Queen sat down to rest on the lake. Suddenly, she became so unbearably sad and lonely that she cried out loudly:

"Oh God, how I want to have a child!" Suddenly the water in the lake began to boil, and a huge shrimp floated out of its depths. She said in a human voice:

"Queen, your dream will come true. But let me, an insignificant shrimp, accompany you to a magical palace that no mortal can see."

"With pleasure!" Replied the Queen. "But I can't swim underwater, as you do." The shrimp laughed and turned into a sweet old lady. When she emerged from the water, her clothes were dry. She was dressed in a white dress with raspberry stripes, and green ribbons were woven into her gray hair. The Queen went after her into a frequent wild forest. The magical path along which they walked shone under their feet, and orange trees weaved the roof over their heads. The divine scent of blooming violets spread all around. After some time, they came to a castle made of pure diamonds.

The castle doors opened, and six beautiful fairies came out to meet the Queen with a bouquet made of precious stones.

"Your Highness," the fairies said, "only a few mortals can visit this palace." Your pleas for the child touched our hearts. You will have a baby named Feif. When he is born, take the bouquet that we have presented to you and pronounce the name of each flower loudly. We will immediately appear and reward your child with the best gifts. The Queen was overjoyed. She thanked the fairy's countless times for their kindness. Then, happy, she went home. After a while, she had a daughter, whom she named Feif. She immediately took out a bouquet and loudly pronounced the name of each flower. And immediately, the whole room was filled with fairies. They were accompanied by little pages carried by caskets with gifts. There were vests and booties, bonnets, and rattles. Everything was embroidered with gold and decorated with precious stones. The fairies played a little with the child and then got to work. In turn, they awarded her with kindness, intelligence, exceptional beauty, luck, and excellent health.

Before the Queen thanked the fairies, the door opened, and a huge shrimp rushed into the room, shouting viciously:

"But you forgot about me!" But you owe this happiness to me. The Queen was horrified.

"Oh, please forgive me," she pleaded.

"I made a terrible mistake!" The fairies joined her:

"Forgive her, please." She did not do this on purpose.

"Well, fine," said the shrimp fairy.

"I will give my child a life. But I warn that before she is fifteen, she should not see daylight; otherwise, something terrible will happen. If you let her see the sun before fifteen, watch out!"

All the windows and doors were boarded up in the royal palace. Nowhere even a ray of light came through. Only candles illuminated the palace rooms. The girl grew up very smart and beautiful. Fairies often came to see her and play with her. She especially fell in love with a fairy named Tulip. She constantly reminded the Queen:

"Remember what the shrimp fairy said. Protect your daughter from daylight." The Queen promised to be careful. When Feif was fourteen years old, the royal painter painted her portrait, and everyone who saw him immediately fell in love with her without memory. At that time, a prince named Wolak lived in another kingdom. He was only 18 years old, and when he saw the portrait of Princess Feif, he was distraught with passion and love. He went to his father, King Sage, and said:

"Father, I need your help. Here is a portrait of Princess Feif. She conquered my heart. Give your blessing. I want to marry her."

"What a beautiful girl, and must be very smart and kind," the king said. "I give you my parental blessing and send Lord Canvis an ambassador to her father." The young Lord Canvis was the prince's closest friend. The prince told him:

"If my life is dear to you, do everything to win the heart of the princess. I will die if she does not become my wife." He gave Canvis a thousand beautiful gifts for the princess. Feif's parents were very flattered when they found out that Prince Wolak was married to their daughter. They knew that this was the best, brave, truthful, and beautiful prince of all that existed in the world. The king and Queen first decided to show Feif to Lord Canvis, but the fairy Tulip warned them that it was unsafe. When the lord arrived at the palace, to his great amazement, he was refused a meeting with the princess. The king told him the whole story of the fairies.

"But, Your Highness," protested Canvis, "Prince Wolak is very much in love. He can neither eat, nor drink, nor sleep. He is very sick. Let me show you his portrait. Understand, if you don't show Prince Feif, he will die of anguish."

"Poor prince," the king said. "He is so madly in love with my daughter. I was also young, and I know what love is. We will try to come up with something." Feif showed a portrait of the prince, and she, too, fell in love with him at first sight. This conversation was heard by Lady Weed, who had two daughters of the same age as Feif. One was called Daisy, and she adored the princess, and the other was called Prikley, and she hated Feif with all her heart. She also saw the portrait of the prince and promised herself to become his wife. Unfortunately, Prikley's godmother was, unfortunately, a shrimp fairy. At night, Prikley went to her and said:

"Feif is getting married to Prince Vaughn. And I want to become his wife. Can you help me with this?"

"Sure! It will be my happiness to upset her dreams," said the evil fairy and whispered something in Prikley's ear. At this time, Feif dreamed of a prince in varnish. Finally, she figured out how to rid him of the disease. She went to her mother and said:

"We can deceive the evil fairy." Send me to the prince in a carriage without windows and with a curtained door. I will go to him at night. The king and Queen agreed with such a plan. They informed Canvis about this, and he, happy, rushed home to tell the Prince the good news. The king ordered a closed carriage to be made. Inside, it was trimmed with green velvet and silver.

The keys to the carriage were handed over to the oldest lord of the kingdom and ordered to be locked in a casket. When everything was ready, Feif, along with Prikley, Daisy, and Lady Weed, got into the carriage. The Queen told Lady Weed:

"I have been handing you the treasure of my whole life. Take care of her; remember that she should not see daylight." The prince had already boarded up the windows in his palace and prepared for the meeting. Weed answered:

"Do not worry and trust me." And they hit the road. After some time, Prikley whispered to her mother:

"Mom, you need to do something urgently. If I do not become the wife of a prince, I will die."

Lady Weed pulled out a long knife which she hid under her skirts, and cut open the carriage upholstery. Daylight surged. Feif immediately turned into a white deer, who jumped out of the carriage and disappeared into the forest. Servants rushed to look for a white deer. But the evil fairy sent a storm on them and carried them all far, far, to the other end of the world. Only Lady Weed, Prikley, and Daisy were left. Prikley put on a Feif engagement ring and her crown.

Soon, they saw the gilded carriage of the prince who was looking forward to his beloved bride. Seeing Prikley, the old king cried out:

"What kind of joke?" Lady Weed answered with dignity:

"This is Princess Feif, Your Highness. And the letters of her father and mother, which I pass on to you, prove this." The prince said:

"Father, they deceived us. The portrait has nothing to do with the original. I'd rather die than marry this freak." The king said:

"Until all the circumstances are clarified, I will take the princess and her attendants as prisoners and put them in the castle." The prince went to his country house in the forest, to hunt and distract from unpleasant thoughts. While walking in the forest, he suddenly felt weak and lay down on the ground. If only he knew that not far from this place, his beloved princess walked, turning into a white deer who loved the light more than anything else. Fairy Tulip knew what happened to Feif. She sent Daisy to look for her beloved princess, and they met, wept bitterly, and hugged.

"My dear princess," said Daisy. "I will stay with you forever and serve you forever."

She took the white deer to the orchard to eat fruits from the trees and asked him where they would spend the night. Indeed, in the forest, there are many wolves, and it is very scary.

"Have you seen any house in this forest?" Daisy asked the deer. He just shook his head. Suddenly, the fairy Tulip appeared, whose heart was touched by the friendship of the girl and the deer, and said:

"Every night, after sunset, Feif will turn back into a girl. Now, follow this path and be brave and patient."

Daisy and the white deer soon arrived at the hut, on the threshold of which an old woman was sitting.

"Will you have a room for me and my deer?" Daisy asked.

"Of course, a young lady," the old woman replied. She led them into a small but very clean room, where two beds stood next to each other. When the sun went down, the white deer turned into a princess who, throwing herself on Daisy's neck, warmly thanked her for her help. They talked all night, and in the morning, Feif again turned into a deer and ran into the forest to pluck grass. At this time, the prince and Lord Canvis came to the same hut in search of an overnight stay. A smiling old woman gave them food and allocated a room, just opposite the girl's room. Having slept, the young prince went hunting. Suddenly he saw a white deer grazing nearby.

Taking aim, he shot a deer, but he, dodging, disappeared into the thicket of the forest. Arriving home in the evening, the deer turned into a princess who told Daisy what had happened to her.

"Sweet princess," said Daisy. "Stay here, don't go to the forest, it's dangerous. I will read books to you, and time will flow quickly."

"I would love to," the princess answered. "But the fact is that when I turn into a deer, I feel like a deer. I have to run and eat grass." Tired, she immediately fell asleep. At this time, in another room, the prince was talking about the wonderful deer that he saw this morning.

"Tomorrow I will definitely shoot him," he said. In the morning, he went in search of a deer. But Feif was on guard and did not leave the thicket of the forest. The prince walked and walked until he fell out of fatigue under an apple tree and fell asleep. At this time, a white deer came out of the thicket and approached the prince.

"He is even more beautiful than in the portrait," Feif thought and lay down beside her. Prince Wolak woke up and was dumbfounded with amazement, next to him lay a white deer. Before he had time to grab the bow, Feif scuttled out of sight. The prince rushed after her and fired. The arrow hit a white deer in the leg, and he fell to the ground.

The prince wanted to shoot him, but when he saw the deer's eyes full of tears and cries, he took pity on him and carried him to the hut. Running out to meet Daisy shouted to him:

"This is my deer! Give it to me!"

"No," the prince answered. "I caught him in the forest. He is mine!"

"I would rather lose my life than my deer," Daisy answered. "Look how he recognizes me now." She said:

"White deer, please give me a leg," and the deer extended his wounded leg. She said:

"White deer, do you love me?" - And the deer nodded his head. The prince was astounded.

"I agree," he said. "The deer is yours. I'm sorry I shot him." Daisy grabbed a deer and carried it to her room. At this time, Lord Canvis told the young prince:

"I recognized this girl, she was accompanied by Princess Feif, I saw her in the princess's carriage. Something is wrong here!" They found out from the old woman in which of the rooms the girls had stopped and made a hole in the wall. Peering into her, they saw Princess Feif sitting on the bed, and next to her Daisy, bandaging her leg. The prince immediately rushed into the girls' room and fell on his knees in front of the princess.

"Forgive me," he cried. "I did not know anything about the deer." I would rather die than do you harm. Feif told him all about her misfortunes.

They talked all night, and the next morning, when the sun rose, the princess suddenly found that this time she had not turned into a deer. Their joy knew no bounds.

"We must inform my father about this," the prince said. "He is going to go to war against your kingdom, accusing your parents of deceit." Suddenly they heard the sounds of the horns and saw that the king himself was coming to them, and Prikley and her mother were sitting in the cattle van.

"My dear father!" - The prince rushed to him.

"Here is my beloved princess Feif. I found her!" He exclaimed. The king glanced at the princess. She stood in a silver dress embroidered with fresh fragrant roses, a crown of diamonds crowned her head. He had never seen such beauty. Not far away stood the Tulip Fairy, who was that old woman by the hut. Everyone was happy. And Lord Canvis, touched by Daisy's devotion and kind heart, made her an offer, and two happy couples married in the palace church. Prikley and her mother were forgiven and sent home. And the whole kingdom has long retold the story of the magical white deer and his adventures, which ended so happily. In the end, take a deep breath in through your nose and slowly and gently breathe out through your mouth. Again, deep breath in and gradually and breathe out one last time, deep breath in and slowly and gently breathe out. Whatever you are ready, wiggle your fingers, wriggle your toes, give a big stretch, and slowly and gently open your eyes. But remember, shine as bright as you can always.

Chapter Six: Princess is Married to the King of the Underworld

Close your eyes and be very still, taking a big deep breath in through your nose and slowly and gently breathe out through your mouth. Take another deep breath in and slowly and gently breathe out through your mouth. One more time, big deep breath in and slowly and gently breathe out through your mouth and relax, feeling peaceful and calm. There was one princess, and she was so beautiful that another such in the world could not be found. She was looking for the same handsome husband. I wandered around the world, everywhere I searched, but could not find it. One day, someone in red pants came to her, a three-cornered hat, a book under her arm. She said:

"You are mine, but I am yours!" He answered her:

"I don't need you if you don't sign in this book!" She cut a finger on her left hand and signed with blood.

He gave her such power that it is only necessary to cross the threshold and, at the same time, think about it, immediately the earth will open, it will go down underground, and the earth will close behind it. So she went to him every day. Father and mother searched for her but did not know where she was disappearing. They ordered to announce that if there is a person who finds out where their daughter goes, they will give her to him as a wife, well, half the kingdom as well. However, no one was announced. One soldier agreed to this offer. He came to the king, and at that time, the princess just came out of the ground. He grabbed her hand and led her to her father. But she told the soldier that she did not want him to clean away. Father was angry with her. He imposed an arrest on her, for which she had no right to leave the room for a month. Once at dinner, servants with a stew lingered.

Father: "Well, where are they with this stew?"

The princess came out, crossed the threshold, and immediately thought that she wanted to her darling. Then she disappeared. The day is passing, there is no daughter anywhere, the week is passing, the daughter is gone, the month is passing, the daughters are gone, and there is not a year, the year has passed, and the daughter has not returned. The king ordered the country to declare that if there is a man who will find his daughter, he will receive her as a wife and half the kingdom. However, there were no volunteers. He ordered the army to declare, and the very soldier who came across the princess when she got out of the ground agreed. He said that he would look for her for three years and that for each year, they would give him a thousand gold. The king paid. A soldier went around the world to look for a princess. He wandered in vain in this world!

He walked through forests, ravines, and cliffs, but knew that he would not find her in the thickets of forests or large cities. Once he made his way through the forest. Suddenly a haze fell, so much so that it did not move. He had to climb a tree. And from a tree nearby, he saw the light. A soldier came to the house in which the light was on. Baba Yaga lived there. And she had one and only maid. The soldier asked for the night, but she did not let go. No matter how he asked, she never agreed that he should spend the night in the house. But she said that there is a well in the yard, so she will lower it into the well on a rope and tie it so that he will spend the night. He allowed the soldier to tie himself with a rope and spent the night in the well. In the morning, as soon as the sun rose, the Baba Yaga of a soldier was pulled out of the well. I gave him breakfast. He thanked her for the night and breakfast. Then he went to the valley. He walked and walked, as long as his legs were carried, until the evening. And where did he end up? Yes, again at the same Baba Yaga. Again, he asked for the night. Not him in the house of Baba Yaga again offered a well. Spent the night the soldier in the well. In the morning, she pulled it out when the sun was already shining. She fed him again. He thanked her for the night and breakfast.

"Yesterday I went that valley, and today I will go another," the soldier decided and walked as much as he could in his legs. From where he went, there he returned again to the same Baba Yaga! Again, I asked for the night, again only in the well did Baba Yaga allow him to spend the night. In the morning, she pulled out, served breakfast, and asked:

31

"Pan soldier, what are you bothering about?"

"I'm looking for such a king's daughter!"

"Why didn't you tell me before? It would be something to bother! I will tell you where she is. Where you spent the night three nights. Because this is not a well, but an abyss into the underworld. I'll let you down!" She began to tie all kinds of ribbons and twine and said:

"Here on this rope, I will lower you. There is a good road at the bottom. The road has two trees and a large house. Go there. There is a pin there. When you find the princess, stick her in the dress. When you want to get up, pull the rope, I will stretch you!" Here she let him down.

He went that way, which the witch pointed to him. I came to a big house. In the first room, there were a lot of guns, in the second, ammunition, in the third, guns, in the fourth room along the wall from top to bottom nails are driven in. On every nail, the human head is suspended. Then he was slightly startled. Entered the fifth room. There, in the middle of the room, a little table stood, round, and on that little table lay a regimental pipe which the soldier put on himself. He left the house and blew the attack. Immediately, officers came to him, an army lined up, saluted to him and shouted:

"What will you order, the most obvious king!" He ordered them nothing, only checked to see if everything was in place. Dismissed them.

A soldier went along one of the tracks, talking to himself:

"What the hell am I the king?" And the devil is behind him:

"Why do you remember me?"

"Where is your princess from another world?" The devil showed him:

"Over there, with our king sits!" The devil immediately ran away, told the king of the underworld that a man had come from the world that the princess was looking for. The king and the princess immediately left for another room and locked themselves. The soldiers could not enter them.

"What can you do?" And then it dawned on him. He took the pipe and began to blow the offensive. The army immediately began to be built, and the officers said to him:

"What do you command us, Mr. King?"

"I will not order anything else, just open me this room, in which the princess sits with the king of the underworld!" Then locksmiths appeared, opened a room, and a soldier entered it. He grabbed the princess by the hand and pulled her away. The king of the underworld cried with burning tears, but could not do anything, because the soldier had a forge.

The whole army accompanied the soldier and princess to that rope. They got in touch, the soldier pulled the rope, and the Baba Yaga pulled them into this world. Baba Yaga asks:

"How did it go? Did he stick a needle in the princess's dress?" The soldier said he had forgotten. Baba Yaga to him:

"Stick in soon. Otherwise, she will leave! Now give me the forge and go home with God, and she will not run away!" So, they got to the house with the princess. The king was pleased when he saw them together. He gave the princess to him as a wife. And this time, the princess was glad of him, because the devil was tired of her. Well, then there was a wedding. In the end, take a deep breath in through your nose and slowly and gently breathe out through your mouth. Again, deep breath in and gradually and breathe out one last time, deep breath in and slowly and gently breathe out. Whatever you are ready, wiggle your fingers, wriggle your toes, give a big stretch, and slowly and gently open your eyes. But remember, shine as bright as you can always.

Chapter Seven: Dancing with the Devils

Close your eyes and be very still, taking a big deep breath in through your nose and slowly and gently breathe out through your mouth. Take another deep breath in and slowly and gently breathe out through your mouth. One more time, big deep breath in and slowly and gently breathe out through your mouth and relax, feeling peaceful and calm. For green forests, for distant lands, one emperor had twelve daughters. The emperor's country was small, and the princesses wanted to live in luxury. Here, to live in luxury, they sold the devil's soul. Princesses always went to a ball somewhere. And at the ball after, each dance, a pair of shoes were thrown away. The emperor was very upset that his daughters did this, no matter how they went to the ball, they would plunder twelve pairs of shoes in one night. The emperor ordered the guard to be put out to find out the soldiers where the princesses go. He caught the guard on guard, stand at the post, and watches. Then the youngest of the princesses brought the soldier a glass. He drank and immediately fell asleep. It was morning; we must go to the report. And he, poor fellow, does not know what happened here. And so it was. The next day, another soldier took up that post. And one of the princesses brought him a glass, and as soon as he drank, he immediately fell asleep, and the princesses picked up and ran to the ball.

The soldier found out nothing again. I came to the report, but he knows nothing. He answered with his head. The third night came. An old soldier joined this post. So, he thought:

"And I can't bear my head!" He had only four cruiser money. With these four cruisers, he set off on a journey. He threw his gun and ran across the wide world, just to save his head. A beggar sat by the road. He asked:

"Where are you going, pan soldier!"

"I'm running wherever my eyes look; otherwise, tomorrow I won't blow my head!" He gave the beggar one cruiser and said:

"Pray for me so that I can escape and keep my head on my shoulders!" I ran further. Met an even more miserable beggar. I thought:

"Since the cruiser gave him that, I will give this two because he is even more unhappy." I ran on. I came across a third beggar. He could not even move. One soldier remained with the soldier; he gave it to the beggar.

And the beggar soldier said:

"Go back to the emperor, do not be afraid! Go to the post. When the princesses give you a drink, you don't drink, pour everything over the collar, and not a drop in your mouth, and pretend that you are sleeping! When the princess pricks you with a needle, do not shout, pretend that you are sleeping!" The beggar soldier obeyed, returned, and stood at the post. He stands at the post. The princess brought him a drink. The soldier obeyed the beggar: he poured booze over the collar and pretended to be sleeping. The princesses came up, pricked him with needles, he endured and pretended to be sleeping. The princesses picked up and to the copper forest. The devils lived there. There they celebrated balls. The soldier is behind them. The Lord helped him. When a soldier ran after the princesses, he met two brothers along the way, and these brothers were pleased to fight. A soldier asked them:

"Why are your brothers fighting?" They told him:

"Our father died. He left us nothing, only a jacket and a pair of boots."

The soldier said to them:

"Why are you brothers fighting over such trifles?" The younger brother answered him:

"Would you, pan soldier, know what kind of jacket this is and what kind of boots! It's such a jacket that you just have to put it on, and nobody will see me, and if you put on your boots, you just have to think about someplace; after a minute, you'll find yourself there!" He did not force to take these things. He told them:

35

"I will judge you!" The soldier took the baton, threw it away, and said:

"Whoever grabs the baton with the first one will get both boots and a jacket!" The brothers again rushed to fight to take possession of the club. And one wanted to grab her, and the other needed her. And the soldier thought:

"This is what I need!" As they fought, he put on his jacket, shod boots, and thought:

"I would get there, where are the princesses!" Immediately there he was. He looked at the ball, but no one saw him in this jacket. The princesses danced, after each dance, the shoes were thrown away, and the soldier collected them.

Suddenly, the younger sister exclaimed:

"Let's go away, then someone is eavesdropping on us and gathers the worn shoes!" The older princess said:

"Then let's go home!" The soldier said to his jacket and boots:

"Run after me to the house until the princesses have returned!" The soldier gathered all the boots and tore one branch in that damn grove through which the princesses ran in front. The soldier lay on a straw mattress and pretended to be sleeping. One princess came, another came, each pricked him. The soldier endured. In the morning, his name is for a report. He said:

"The clearest pan! I found out, but not everything!"

"Wait, you'll go tomorrow and find out!" The soldier arrives the next day. Princesses come, bring him a glass, he lets everything out of the collar. The princesses prick him again, they say whether he is sleeping, and he pretends to be sleeping.

He thought:

"Jacket, put on so that they don't see me, and you, boots, follow the princesses!" He came there, they dance again, and he collects his worn

36

boots. When he collected all the shoes, he set off home again, and again, on the way, picked one branch in the forest. The morning came; the soldier came to the report.

"How did you watch?"

"Pan emperor, your daughters are dancing with the devil, here you have their shoes, which they have trampled on dancing, and they are dancing in the grove from which I brought you two branches." And the emperor told him:

"Since you are so brave, I will give one of the princesses to you as a wife." And the soldier answered him like this:

"It's better I'll take the poor, but the devout than the rich who knows the devil!" In the end, take a deep breath in through your nose and slowly and gently breathe out through your mouth. Again, deep breath in and gradually and breathe out one last time, deep breath in and slowly and gently breathe out. Whatever you are ready, wiggle your fingers, wriggle your toes, give a big stretch, and slowly and gently open your eyes. But remember, shine as bright as you can always.

Chapter Height: The Poor and Wise Princess

Once upon a time, there was a king, and he had a daughter, young and beautiful and so wise and reasonable that she had no equal in the whole district, and the glory of her wisdom reached even the ninth kingdom. The king persuaded her to choose a groom and hurried with the wedding. Only the princess didn't want to think about the wedding, and all were discouraged:

"Sovereign, you are my father, do not persuade me, I do not want to get married." But the king insisted, and the beautiful princess finally agreed:

"Good," she said. "As you wish. Only I have one condition. My husband will be the one who will ask me a riddle that I will not guess. And whoever dares me to solve the riddle that I will guess, order him to be executed." The king thought:

"Pain in your wisdom, do not brag. You have a wise head, but you will still find a fellow that you will be wiser." And he agreed with everything that the princess had in mind. From all sides, from far and near lands, grooms, nobles and peasants, rich and poor, old and young, began to gather. Only none of them managed to puzzle the princess with a riddle that she would not have guessed. And to each of them, the executioner chopped off his head. The king even turned gray with all this, but there was nothing left for him to do. In one village, a poor widow lived with her son. And she had no one but this song and even a couple of pigeons. And the son was in his twentieth year, and he was a handsome and handsome young man. So, he once said to his mother:

"I'll go and make a mystery for the royal daughter."

Mother only threw up her hands. She begged him, asked, and invoked to forget her invention and not risk her young life in vain. Only everything was in vain; the son did not convince. He stood his ground. And as she saw that he was going to the princess, she decided that it would be better to take his life from herself than to give the executioner for reproach. She agreed for the sake of visibility and baked the son of two pigeons on the road. And she poisoned these pigeons. The fellow went on a journey, and after him, the neighbor's dog ran, hairy and shaggy. They walked along, and the fellow noted that the dog barely moved his legs from hunger. He threw him two baked pigeons. The dog ate pigeons and immediately fell to the ground dead. Well done, the dog left lying on the road and went on. Then suddenly the road disappeared. He stopped in indecision and then returned.

He comes again to the place where he left the dead dog, and instead of the dead dog, there are twelve dead ravens. Gathered well-done ravens and went on. Soon night fell, and the widow's son decided to spend the night in the forest. At midnight a gang of robbers came into the forest, and there were only twenty-four of them. They caught the young man and took him to their refuge. And the young man pulled out the dead ravens, plucked them, cut off their legs and heads, roasted them, and gave each of the robbers a half. No sooner had the robbers of the ravens eat; they immediately fell dead. On the second day, the fellow went on. This time he did not have to go long. He went out of the woods to the plain and saw a large city from a distance, and in the middle of that city on a high hill, a royal castle. He began to think, what riddle to the princess. He thought, though, and finally decided to ask her if she would guess what happened to him on the road.

He came to the royal castle and ordered the king to report about himself. The king led him to the princess, who was already waiting for him on the throne, surrounded by court ladies. The young man boldly appeared before the princess, and when she asked him to make a riddle, he began:

"Two dead killed a living one, and that living one, when he died, killed twelve more, and that twelve dead killed twenty-four more. And only the one who killed the first two survived. What is it?"

The royal daughter thought, though, in all the books in which riddles from around the world were collected, she looked for the answer, and in the courtyard, the royal executioner was already sharpening an ax. Only in vain did the princess break her head; in vain did the executioner sharpen the ax. She had to admit that she did not know how to answer the riddle, and she asked the young man to tell the answer herself. The young man agreed and said:

"As I gathered at your palace, my mother did not want to let me go. And she decided with her own hands to take my life, so as not to give the executioner a shame. So, she baked two pigeons and gave them on the road. On the way, I gave the pigeons to a hungry dog, and he immediately died. Twelve ravens flew to that dog, and all died too. And the twelve poisoned ravens ate twenty-four robbers. This is what happened to me on the way to the castle."

The royal daughter had to surrender, and that very evening the poor man became her husband. The king ordered a feast all over the world, and when everyone ate and drank, he punched the table with his fist and said that he had never had so much fun. In the end, take a deep breath in through your nose and slowly and gently breathe out through your mouth. Again, deep breath in and gradually and breathe out one last time, deep breath in and slowly and gently breathe out. Whatever you are ready, wiggle your fingers, wriggle your toes, give a big stretch, and slowly and gently open your eyes. But remember, shine as bright as you can always.

Chapter Nine: King Ram

Close your eyes and be very still, taking a big deep breath in through your nose and slowly and gently breathe out through your mouth. Take another deep breath in and slowly and gently breathe out through your mouth. One more time, big deep breath in and slowly and gently breathe out through your mouth and relax, feeling peaceful and calm. Once upon a time, there was a king, and he had three daughters. All of them were very beautiful, but the youngest was more beautiful than all. Her name was Wanda, and she was her father's favorite. She was always given the most gifts and the least forbidden to play pranks. Once the king went to war. Hearing that he had won and was returning home, the daughters dressed up for his arrival: the eldest wore a green dress with emeralds, the middle one was blue with turquoise, and the youngest was white with diamonds. The joyful king returned, and the feast began.

Having called the eldest daughter, the father asked her:

"Tell me why you put on a green dress?"

"Your Majesty, I heard about your great victory and put on a green dress to show my pride in your courage and happiness for your happy return."

"Well said," the king smiled. "And you, my average, why in blue today?"

"Your Majesty, I put on a blue dress to show how we worried about you. Your return is like a clear blue sky on a sunny day."

"Fine," said the king. "And you, dear Wanda, why did you choose white?"

"Because he suits me," the princess answered. "And just that?" Asked the disappointed king. He was very selfish and temperamental, and he liked it when his daughters worshiped him.

"Do you have another reason?"

"Father, my reason is to be as attractive as possible. We, your daughters, love you and must do everything to please your gaze."

"Truly a smart answer!" - Exclaimed the king. – "And now tell me what you dreamed about last night."

The first daughter said that she dreamed that her father brought her a dress woven with gold and precious stones.

The middle one is that he gave her a golden buckle with silver knitting needles. And the youngest one said:

"I dreamed about the wedding day of my middle sister, and you, father, called me and said: Come, I will wash your hands with rose water." An enraged king jumped up from the throne:

"This damsel is stupid and proud! She thinks that I can be her servant, and yet I am the king!" He called the guard and ordered:

"You heard everything. See what intrigues Wanda weaves? Take her to a dense forest and chop it into pieces. And in proof of death, bring me her heart and tongue."

The guards were terrified, but they were afraid of the king and promised that they would fulfill his order exactly. Then, seizing the princess, they led her into the forest.

Seeing tears in the eyes of the guards, the princess asked:

"Did something happen? Tell me; I will try to help."

"Madam, we have been given a terrible task; your father ordered you to be killed." Wanda turned pale.

"Did he order to kill me? I know you since childhood and have not done anything wrong. I love and honor my father."

"Madam, we cannot kill you, but we also cannot leave you here. Run, and we will try to deceive your father." Wanda thanked the guards and hurried

43

into the forest. She walked and walked until midnight arrived. Tree branches tore her clothes and scratched her face. She felt mortal fatigue and hunger. Stopping, she heard the bleating of a sheep in the distance.

"Maybe it's a forester's cabin? She thought. I'll try to ask them for clothes because mine has torn to shreds, and I still have a long way to go." She headed toward the sheep's voice and soon came to a large corral. There on the carpet of fragrant flower petals stood a huge snow-white ram, adorned with a gold chain with precious stones. A golden tent towered above him, and around him were hundreds of decorated sheep and rams. Instead of grass, they ate strawberry ice cream with chocolate cream and washed down with lemonade. Not far away were two card tables, at which the sheep played poker. The amazed princess froze on the threshold. King Ram invited her to enter.

"Tell me what brought you to us."

"I had to run away from home because my father wanted to kill me."

"Stay with us," the ram said sympathetically. Servant rams brought a huge pumpkin. It was hollowed out from the inside and trimmed with snow-white velvet. King Ram took Wanda's hand and helped enter her inside. Then the rams picked up the pumpkin and carried it to the high hill where the cave was located. King Ram opened the door with a key.

"Don't be scared, princess, and follow me." Step by step, they went down the spiral staircase into the depths of the cave, and suddenly a magical garden opened in front of them, full of flowers and sparkling fountains. Instead of water, they had overseas drinks. Outlandish fruits hung on the trees, and besides, savory ham, freshly fried chickens, nosy cheese and fragrant crayfish swayed on the branches. The flower petals were made of chocolate and caramel. All food was as if specially prepared for their arrival. Along the alley stood golden houses strewn with precious stones. Choosing the most beautiful, King Ram said:

"Here you can live in peace. Your every desire will be immediately fulfilled."

"How kind you are to me, Your Majesty," the princess answered, "but I am so unusual here that I would rather return home."

"Remain at least to listen to my story," King Ram asked.

"I am the son of a wealthy and noble king. Once on a hunt, my servants fell behind me. I went to the edge of the forest and saw a lake with clear water. Approaching him to get drunk, I suddenly discovered that the water in the lake was hot, not cold. While I was meditating looking at the water, a pillar of fire suddenly soared from the middle of the lake, which, taking me, carried it along with me. At the bottom of the lake, I saw an evil fairy named Ragtag. She, seeing me, cried out: "Now you will be my captive, I will turn you into a ram!" With a wave of a magic wand, she turned me into my present form. All the sheep and rams around her are also her captives. These are unfortunate kind people who once angered this little man."

Wanda was surprised to hear his story and agreed to stay with her. Soon, she noticed that King Ram was not only pleasant but also very smart.

He sincerely loved her, and his feeling did not go unanswered. He told her that he hoped one day to become a man again, and then he would take her to his kingdom, where they would live happily together. They hunted, played music, and chatted about everything in the world. So, some time has passed. Once, the princess heard the news that her older sister was getting married.

"Oh, how I would like to see this wedding," Wanda dreamed.

"We can easily do this!" — said King Ram.

"But promise me to go back." Wanda promised, and at that very moment, she ended up in her father's palace. All the courtiers, not recognizing her, were perplexed: who is this rich beauty? The father king also did not recognize her because he was sure that his daughter died many years ago. After the marriage ceremony, she disappeared. The king was saddened by this and ordered his servants:

"As soon as the stranger appears again, close her in the throne room. I want to know who she is."

After a while, Wanda's second sister decided to get married. Wanda again asked King Ram to let her go home.

"I promise you," she said, "to return here immediately." After the wedding ceremony, she was about to leave for home, but, to her horror, found that all the doors were locked. Suddenly the king came in and said:

"Do not be afraid of beauty. I want you to stay with the other guests at the banquet. I'll go and wash your hands with rose water."

Wanda suddenly remembered her dream, which caused her unhappiness, and cried out:

"You see, father, the dream has come true, and this made no one sick."

The king fell at her feet and began to pray for forgiveness. He told her:

"You are very wise." Be the Queen instead of me! Everyone was happy, and the feast lasted many days. Meanwhile, King Ram waited and waited for Princess Wanda, and finally realized that she would not return.

"I'm too ugly, she left forever," he cried. "But I can't live without her. Oh, the evil fairy, why did you enchant me!" He wandered sadly to the palace of Wanda's father. A guard at the gate beat him with a stick. He fell in longing at the palace gates and died. Wanda forgot about the joy of meeting with her family for a moment. She laughed, sang, and danced. Suddenly, my father invited everyone to go to the palace gates and enjoy the fireworks. When they approached them, Wanda suddenly, with horror, saw the lifeless body of her beloved ram on the ground.

She ran to him and began to kiss him, but he did not wake up; he was dead. She wept bitterly, realizing that she had lost her lover forever. So, one day, our joy goes away, replaced by sadness. In the end, take a deep breath in through your nose and slowly and gently breathe out through your mouth. Again, deep breath in and gradually and breathe out one last time, deep

46

breath in and slowly and gently breathe out. Whatever you are ready, wiggle your fingers, wriggle your toes, give a big stretch, and slowly and gently open your eyes. But remember, shine as bright as you can always.

Chapter Ten: The Fool Who Wanted to Marry a Princess

Close your eyes and be very still, taking a big deep breath in through your nose and slowly and gently breathe out through your mouth. Take another deep breath in and slowly and gently breathe out through your mouth. One more time, big deep breath in and slowly and gently breathe out through your mouth and relax, feeling peaceful and calm. One mother had three sons, two smart and one fool. And the daughter of the king of that country fell ill, she was sad and the king said that he would marry her to someone who could make her laugh. Three brothers had an apple orchard. And one of the smart ones said:

"I will amuse her." He took the basket, went to the garden, plucked three apples, put them in the basket, and hit the road. An older woman met him in a grove.

"What are you talking about?" She asked.

"Horse dung," the guy answered.

"It will be so!" The older woman mumbled. A smart guy came to the palace, and there they set a guard at the entrance and ordered her to let everyone who was going to make the princess laugh. But the princess was not sick, and she was just bewitched. The wise guy said what he needed, and the guard missed him. He stood in front of the king, and the king said:

"Go to my daughter, try to make her laugh."

The guy went into the chambers of the princess and knocked over the basket. But instead of apple horse manure sprinkled out of it. Then the king ordered the clever man to be beaten off, and the clever man trudged home, hanging his head, all bruised. Mother asked:

"What happened to you?"

"Nothing," the son answered, "they chopped me off; that's all." And he told his mother what the apples had turned into. This was heard by a second smart brother and said:

"I'll go down to the orchard for apples." And he also plucked three apples. Seeing him on the road, his mother said:

"Look, it wouldn't have happened to you that with your brother."

"Well, no," the son answered and went to the palace. Passing through the grove, he met an older woman, and she asked:

"What are you talking about, son?"

"Seashells," the guy answered.

"Shells will be!" The older woman mumbled. He came to the palace, and they let him in. When the guy was brought to the princess's chambers, he emptied the basket, and shells sprinkled out of it. The princess was even sadder, and the king ordered the clever man to be beaten with sticks. And he trudged home, too, all bruised.

He told his mother that he could not make the princess laugh and that he was beaten off cool. It remained now a fool to try his luck. And he said:

"I will make her laugh." He took a basket and went into the garden for apples. The brothers warned him:

"There is nothing left!" But he nevertheless went, began to search and found the last, most beautiful apple, and it hung in the thick of branches. The guy put it in a basket and hit the road. An older woman met him in a grove and asked:

"What are you talking about, son?"

And the fool answered: "Apple."

"Well then, an apple will be an apple." He came to the palace and said that he was going to make the princess laugh, but the guard did not let him go.

49

So, the king ordered, because everyone who came only upset the princess, and she was completely alienated. The fool began to beg the guards. The people crowding around, also asked for him, and finally, they let him into the king, and the king led the guy to the princess. The fool turned the basket over, and the apple fell to the floor. And then the girl laughed and amused, it was painfully beautiful, this apple. Then the king said:

"You will marry a pointless." But in three days you have to build a ship that can walk on land and water.

A fool went into the grove, met an older woman there again, and began to cry bitterly. And the older woman asked him:

"What happened to you, son?"

And the fool said that he freed the princess from evil spells, but the king ordered him to build a ship in three days, which will walk on water and land.

"Do not be sad, son!" Said the older woman.

"Get yourself an ax, a saw, and a hammer. Everything will be done on time."

For two days, he searched for an ax, a saw, and a hammer, and on the third brought them to the older woman. And suddenly a ship appeared in front of him. The fool boarded the ship and sailed through the grove. When the third day was running out, the ship was already standing at the palace. The king was amazed and said:

"You executed my order. I will give you my daughter as your wife, only before you took care of two hundred rabbits for three days. At least one will run away, you will not see the princess, and you will say goodbye to life. So, I give you three days, guards."

The fool went into the grove and began to cry bitterly. An older woman appeared and asked:

"What is the matter with you, son?" And he said that he had three days to watch two hundred rabbits. If even one escapes, the king executes him.

Then the old woman said:

"Here is a pipe for you. You'll play, the rabbits will run to you, and no one will leave. Just be careful - there you will guard them, and they will ask you to sell rabbits, but you should never sell them."

The fool brought the pipe to his mouth and was about to follow the rabbits. And the older woman warned him:

"To everyone who wants to buy a rabbit, say what you sell for a kiss."

And the fool went to watch the rabbits. He played the pipe, and not a single rabbit ran away. The first servant of the king came to buy rabbits. The fool told her:

"I do not sell rabbits."

"Well, please sell at least one!" - said the maid.

"Kiss me, and I'll give you a rabbit," the fool suggested.

"Good," she agreed. The maid kissed him, and he gave her a rabbit. She left, but when she began to approach the palace, the fool played on the pipe, and the rabbit ran to him. In the palace, the king asked:

"Why didn't you bring the rabbit?"

"He doesn't want to sell," the maid answered. The next day, the royal daughter came for the rabbit.

"If you kiss me," said the fool,

"I will give you a rabbit."

"Good," the girl agreed. She kissed him, and he gave her a rabbit. But when the princess approached the palace, the fool played on the pipe, and the rabbit ran away. In the palace, the king asked his daughter why she had not brought a rabbit.

"He doesn't want to sell," said the princess. Then the servant of the king volunteered:

"I will go." He came to the fool, and he said:

"If you kiss my forehead, I will give you a rabbit."

The servant did so, took the rabbit, and left. When he approached the palace, the fool began to play the pipe, and the rabbit returned. The king asks where the rabbit is. And the servant replied:

"He does not want to sell." Then the queen volunteered:

"Now I will go. She came to the fool and asked to sell a rabbit. And he replied:

"I do not sell rabbits. But if you kiss me, so be it, I will give you one."

And the queen kissed the fool and took the rabbit. But when she approached the palace, he played on the pipe, and the rabbit ran back. The king saw that she came empty-handed, was angry and said:

"Now, I will go myself." He came to the fool and asked to sell a rabbit. He replied that he did not sell rabbits, but he could give one of the kings kissed his forehead. And the king kissed his forehead and got a rabbit. But when the king approached the palace, the fool played on the pipe, and the rabbit returned to him. And then the king said:

"He will have to give him a daughter, anyway, he has already kissed with our whole family." And the fool married a princess. In the end, take a deep breath in through your nose and slowly and gently breathe out through your mouth. Again, deep breath in and gradually and breathe out one last time, deep breath in and slowly and gently breathe out. Whatever you are ready, wiggle your fingers, wriggle your toes, give a big stretch, and slowly and gently open your eyes. But remember, shine as bright as you can always.

Chapter Eleven: Blue Crest

Close your eyes and be very still, taking a big deep breath in through your nose and slowly and gently breathe out through your mouth. Take another deep breath in and slowly and gently breathe out through your mouth. One more time, big deep breath in and slowly and gently breathe out through your mouth and relax, feeling peaceful and calm. In one kingdom, there was a widowed king. He was incredibly rich, and he had a daughter, whose name was April, and she was more beautiful than spring. When she was 15 years old, her father married again. The stepmother had a daughter, whose name was Trotti, and she was worse than the worst night. Her face was like the cracked skin of a drum, her hair was like tangled yarn, and her body was yellow like old wax. But the stepmother adored her daughter and wished her every happiness. Once the king said:

"Perhaps the time has come to marry our daughters."

"It's a great idea," the queen replied.

"My daughter deserves the most beautiful and wealthiest husband in the world." She, unlike the stupid April, is smart and attractive. And since she is older than April, she must be the first to get married. The king agreed because he was kind and did not like scandals. He invited King Crispin, the most influential and wealthy in the world, to the palace. Meanwhile, the queen bought up all the matter in the city and found Trotti many outfits. She burned the remaining material. Thus, April had to be content with old outfits. On that day, when Crispin was waiting for the arrival, the queen persuaded an evil maid, and she doused with mud and tore all April's clothes to shreds. Therefore, the princess was forced to hide in the darkest corner, and from there, watch Crispin. Crispin was introduced to Trotti. Dressed in velvet and lace, she looked even uglier than ever. Backing away from her, King Crispin said:

"Do you still have a princess? I heard her name is April."

"Yes, here she is," said Trotti, pointing a finger at the princess who was hiding in a corner. The king looked at her and immediately fell in love without memory. He talked with her for three whole hours and, to his indescribable joy, became convinced that she was as smart as she was beautiful.

The enraged queen and Trotti came to the king's father with a demand to immediately imprison April in the fortress. The king, under his wife's heel, agreed. At this time, Crispin, returning home, constantly dreamed of a princess. The Queen, sneaking into his kingdom and endowing his servants with gold, told them to tell Crispin all sorts of nasty things about April. One of the servants told him that she likes to kill cats and dogs, the other—that she is a witch and flies on a broom at night, the third—that she is crazy. But Crispin did not listen to their lies. He came to April's kingdom, hoping to see her again. But she was nowhere to be found. Sorry, Crispin demanded an answer.

"Her father imprisoned her, where she will be until her sister marries," the queen answered him. Crispin immediately called his faithful servant to him and told him:

"It's about my life. I want you to find out where Princess April is."

The servant recognized and reported to his master. The Queen overheard this conversation, and her cunning plan was born. She replaced April and put Trotti in prison instead. In the dark of the night, the king in love made his way to the dungeon and, falling at the prisoner's feet, made love to her and asked her for consent to marry him. As a sign of his sincere love, he put Trotti on his finger (thinking it was April) a wedding ring. They agreed to meet again tomorrow. When the next night came, even darker than the previous one, King Crispin drove up to the dungeon in a carriage drawn by fast-footed horses and helped Trotti get out of the window. He put her in a carriage, and they rushed to his palace. He was sure that he was abducting April. On the way, he asked where she wanted to marry him. Trotti replied that her godmother, the fairies, was Fretful. The king agreed, and they drove to the castle of the evil fairy.

Trotti rushed inside and, throwing herself to her godmother's neck, told her everything, praying for help. The fairy went out to meet the king and said:

"Here is my godmother, Princess Trotti, you told her that you love her and want to marry her. Keep your promise."

"What?!" Cried the furious king. "Should I marry this stupid freak? Never and never! She is cheating, claiming that I promised to marry her. Let it prove it!"

"And here is the proof, stupid king," said Trotti, showing the engagement ring.

"You put it on my finger."

"This is a lie!" - shouted the king. "And I will prove it!" Trotti and the fairy insisted on getting married, begged him, and threatened, but he was adamant. So, they argued twenty days and nights. Finally, the tired fairy said:

"Crispin, choose one of two things: either I will conjure you for your disobedience, or you will marry my goddaughter." Crispin answered:

"Do what you want, but only April will be my wife." And at that moment, he turned into a small bird with thin blue feathers. A small blue tuft stuck out on her head like a crown.

"Fine," said the evil fairy.

"You will be a bird for exactly seven years, and now fly away, the window is open." The king flew away from the witching place, his only desire was to find April and ask her to wait seven long years, until he again turns into a man, and they get married. The fairy sent Trotti back to her mother. When the queen found out that her plan had failed, she was completely distraught.

"I will avenge April for this," she hissed. Having conceived a new, even more sophisticated plan, she put Trotti on the queen's crown and brought her to April.

"Here is your sister," she said, "she has just returned from her wedding. Now she is the wife of King Crispin." And Trotti showed poor April the king's engagement ring. Screaming from anguish, the princess fell unconscious, and when she woke up, she asked:

"Leave me alone, I have already sipped enough grief. I no longer have the strength to live." All the following days and nights, she sat at the dungeon window, yearning and crying. Meanwhile, the poor king flew around the palace in the hope of a huge citrus tree growing next to the dungeon window. A blue bird crouched on a branch of this tree to rest. Suddenly she heard a dreary voice begging for death.

Recognizing this dearest voice in the whole world, the bird flew up to April's window:

"Don't be sad, my dear princess."

"Who are you?" - The princess exclaimed in amazement, looking at a beautiful blue bird speaking in a human voice.

"Princess, I am ready to give my life for you," said the strange bird, "Didn't you recognize me? I am King Crispin. Fairy Fretful turned me into a bird for seven years, but this cannot change my love for you."

"How can this be? Brave King Crispin in the world turned into such a small bird?"

"This is the price I paid for loving you."

"Love? If you loved me, you would never marry Trotti. I saw your ring on her finger."

"Trotti said I married her? She is lying! They want to make you forget me. They tricked me into the palace, and then offered me a choice: either to become a bird or to marry your sister." April realized that Crispin was telling the truth.

She was so glad to see him that she immediately forgot about her bondage. They talked all night, and in the morning, they were forced to leave so that no one would see them, promising each other to meet at the window every night. To prove April's love, Crispin flew into the castle and brought her a pair of diamond earrings as a gift. The next night, he presented her with a bracelet adorned with a huge emerald. Then he gave her a watch made of a huge pearl. Every day he flew to the palace and brought unusual gifts to the princess. April soon had a huge collection of jewels. At night she put them on herself to please Crispin, and during the day, she hid them in caskets. Two years have passed. April was no longer burdened with imprisonment: every night, she met her beloved. Meanwhile, her stepmother continued to try to marry Trotti. Envoys were sent to all parts of the country, but as soon as Trotti's name was mentioned, they were sent back.

The Queen thought it was April's fault, and she hated her more and more every day. One night, he and Trotti went to the fortress to speak with April. Approaching the door, they heard a bird's voice.

"Trotti, she is deceiving us!" - The queen shouted and burst into the room. Faster than lightning, April closed the window, giving the bird a chance to escape.

"Who are you talking to at night?" The queen hissed viciously.

"Not with anyone," April replied calmly, "I don't see anyone here except the servants you are sending me." But the queen and Trotti did not listen to her; they looked in all eyes at sparkling diamonds.

"Where did you get these jewels?"

"I found them here."

"Oh, you are a liar! We'll teach you a lesson now," said Trotti.

"It's not time yet," the queen put in.

"Maybe she got these diamonds from her good fairy mother. Punishing her, we will anger the fairy." They sent the girl to serve April and strictly ordered her to look after everything that happens in the dungeon.

April understood their plan and did not go to the window, despite the fact that she saw a blue bird spinning behind him, yearning. For a month, the servant, without closing her eyes, watched April. Finally, she fell asleep. The princess hurried to the window and sang: Blue bird, blue as the sky and the sea, faster, fly to me faster! Crispin immediately appeared. They talked all night. Over the next two nights, the maid continued to sleep, and the happiness of the lovers did not interfere. But the next night she woke up and pretended to be sleeping. The light of the moon fell on the princess, talking with a blue bird.

At dawn, the bird flew away, and the maid immediately went to report on this queen.

"That must be Crispin," concluded Trotti.

"How dare they lead us like that?" The queen cried.

"Now it is our turn." She told the maid to pretend as if nothing had happened. That night, April sang her song again, but no one arrived. The evil queen ordered to cut down a citrus tree, and, unfortunately, Crispin fell under the blow of an ax. His legs and wings were hurt. He was dying. Crispin longed for death, thinking that April had betrayed him by telling the queen about his nightly visits. Fortunately, he had a wizard friend who continued to search for him for all these long years. Eight times he went around the world in search of his beloved king. Now for the ninth time, he passed by the place where Crispin lay.

"Oh, where are you, dear Crispin?" He called out. And suddenly from the ground, the friend's weak voice answered him:

"I'm here, look under the citrus tree."

The wizard looked but saw only a wounded blue bird.

"It's me, Crispin, an evil sorceress has enchanted me," the bird whispered. The wizard grabbed her in his arms and quietly uttered a few magic words. And Crispin got better. He told a friend about everything that happened to him. And about April's betrayal.

"What a crappy girl," the wizard said, "forget her. She's not worth your love. Now I can't return your appearance to you, but soon, I hope I will be able to do it."

"Put me in a birdcage," the king asked.

"Of course," the wizard answered, "but your kingdom cannot do without a king for five whole years. We must definitely come up with something." Meanwhile, April called all day at the window of Crispin. She was very afraid that Trotti and the Queen killed the bird. She tried to question them, but they were silent, thereby tormenting her heart even more. Father April was seriously ill at the time. When he died, the kingdom passed to Trotti and her mother. Evil by nature, they tormented and tormented everyone around. The queen died of malice, and Trotti hurried to her godmother, fleeing the vengeance of those around her.

People freed April from prison and solemnly crowned her. Even as a queen, April thought all day about Crispin. Once, leaving a Lord Advisor in her place, she put on all her jewelry donated by him and went in search of her beloved bird. The wizard made every effort to turn Crispin into a man, but he did not succeed. Finally, he decided to go to Fretful and try to negotiate with her. He invited her to return Crispin a human appearance, and in return, he promised to persuade Crispin to think about marrying Trotti. Fretful agreed. She dressed Trotti in silver and gold and sent it to Crispin. Seeing her again, the king could not contain his disgust. Day after day passed, and he hated her more and more. Meanwhile, April, dressed as a poor peasant woman, was looking for him everywhere. Once, sitting by a stream, she was resting in the shade of trees. Suddenly, an elderly woman appeared out of nowhere and asked:

"What are you doing here, dear?"

"I'm looking for a blue bird," the sad April answered and told her story. Suddenly, an old woman turned into a beautiful sorceress.

"Amiable April," she said, "My sister Fretful has already cast a spell on Crispin. He is in his palace, and if you are brave, your story will have a happy

60

ending. Here are four eggs for you. When disaster strikes you, break one of them, help will come from there."

April thanked the sorceress and hurried to the palace to Crispin. Seven days and nights later, she reached the huge crystal mountain. No matter how she tried to get on it, everything was useless. Finally, she remembered the testicles and broke one of them. Inside, she found small golden spikes, which she attached to the slippers and easily climbed the mountain. But how to get down? She broke the second testicle. From there, a carriage pulled by two pigeons fell out. In front of April, the carriage became large. April got into it and asked:

"Little birds, please get me home soon to the kingdom of Crispin." A few minutes later, the carriage stopped at the gate. Having smeared her face with soot so that no one would recognize her, April asked the guards where she could find the king.

"Tonight, he will publicly announce his engagement to Princess Trotti," they said. April's heart ached:

"Trotti! While I am worried about him, he decided to marry this stupid freak. He forgot all his promises!" And she went to the royal square. Soon there appeared Trotti, richly dressed, but even uglier than before. April went up to her.

"Who is this dirty peasant woman who gets my dress dirty?" Cried Trotti.

"I brought you a present," April said and took out an emerald bracelet donated by Crispin. Trotti's eyes glittered eagerly.

"I'll give you fifty cents for him," she suggested.

"Show it to the appraisers, and then we can talk about the price," April said. Trotti eagerly ran to the king. He was surprised to see a familiar bracelet.

"I know only one bracelet in the world, but maybe two of them. Buy it." Trotti returned to April.

"How much do you want for him?"

"All the gold of the world is not enough for you. But if you want, you can keep it for yourself in exchange for a night spent in the room above the royal bedchamber."

"And just that," Trotti rejoiced. The fact was that everything that was said in this room was heard in the bedroom. And everything that was done in the bedroom was heard in this room. Late at night, standing in the middle of the room, April said:

"Have you really forgotten me? After all, you swore to me in love, and now Trotti has taken my place." The servants heard this, but the king did not. Because since he left April, Crispin took sleeping pills every night. April did not know what to think when she did not hear the answer. In desperation, she broke the third egg. Inside it was a golden carriage driven by a small mouse. Instead of a horse, there was a big gray cat. Four little clowns sat inside. In the evening, April showed Trotti this little thing.

"How much do you want for her?"

"You can't buy it for money. Let me spend another night in the same room." Greedy Trotti agreed. That night, April reminded the king of their former happy days, but her words went unanswered. The king was fast asleep. In desperation, April broke the fourth egg. Four small toy birds flew out. They could sing like alive; they could predict the fate and were knowledgeable in medicine. As soon as April left the room, the servants said to her:

"Is that how you make noise in the room above the royal bedroom? It's good that the king takes sleeping pills and does not hear you. And he would certainly drive you away." April finally understood why Crispin was not responding to her.

She took all her jewels out of her bag and suggested to the servants:

"If today, instead of sleeping pills, you give the king regular pills, all of this will be yours." The servants agreed. Then the princess went to Trotti and showed her magic birds.

"How much do they cost?"

"The fee is the same." The night has come. April whispered by the window:

"I suffered so many misfortunes. I abandoned the kingdom and my people. Have you really forgotten me?"

At first, Crispin thought he was raving. He shouted:

"This is a cruel dream, reminding me of the princess who betrayed me." And then April told him about everything that had happened. The happy king ran into the room and fell at her feet, begging for forgiveness. Trotti, who appeared in the room, saw this and died of anger. And King Crispin and Princess April got married and lived together happily for many, many years. In the end, take a deep breath in through your nose and slowly and gently breathe out through your mouth. Again, deep breath in and gradually and breathe out one last time, deep breath in and slowly and gently breathe out. Whatever you are ready, wiggle your fingers, wriggle your toes, give a big stretch, and slowly and gently open your eyes. But remember, shine as bright as you can always.

Chapter Twelve: Hans and the Tabby Cat

Close your eyes and be very still, taking a big deep breath in through your nose and slowly and gently breathe out through your mouth. Take another deep breath in and slowly and gently breathe out through your mouth. One more time, big deep breath in and slowly and gently breathe out through your mouth and relax, feeling peaceful and calm. Once upon a time, there was a lonely miller who had three students. Earlier, he called them to his place to talk about something important.

"As you know, I have no children," he said.

"Therefore, I want one of you to inherit the mill. It will go to the one who finds and brings me the most beautiful horse in the world. Go and come back with horses in seven years." The youngest student was called Hans. He was lazy and stupid to such an extent that everyone just laughed at him.

"Where did you go with us," the senior students told him.

"If you even get the mill, you don't know how to manage it." But Hans did not answer, and stubbornly followed them. At night, when Hans fell asleep, the brothers ran away from him. Waking up, Hans was distraught:

"What should I do now?" He wailed. "I cannot find the horse myself alone." Suddenly he saw a tabby cat sitting in his head, asking him in a human voice:

"Where are you going, dear Hans?"

"To tell you the truth, I don't know," answered Hans.

"Well, then I offer you this. Come with me, promise to obey me for precisely seven years, and after this period I will give you the most beautiful horse in the world."

"I agree," said Hans. "If you are so smart that you can speak in a human voice, then I think I can rely on you."

The cat brought Hans to his palace, where many servants washed him, changed his clothes, and fed him fantastic food. After that, they took him to a luxurious room and laid him in a silk-white bed. Every day, Hans carefully followed all the cat's orders: he chopped a bush with a silver ax, watered a rose from a golden watering can in the garden, cut the forest with diamond scissors. Once, noticing that his clothes became cramped and his shoes were worn out, he thought:

"Have you been seven years already?" and he asked the cat in the evening:

"Dear cat, I don't know how much time I have with you, but is it time for me to get my promised horse already?"

"It's not time yet," the cat replied.

"First, you will have to build a house. Here you have silver nails, a hammer, and boards. Build everything from silver!"

"Good," Hans answered, and set to work. When he did everything, the cat was satisfied, and, having thanked him, he led the stable to choose a horse that he liked. But all the horses were so good that he could not select the best.

"We will do it like this," said the cat.

"You go to the mill, and in three days I will bring you the horse myself," Hans said goodbye to the cat, dressed in his old ragged clothes and went home.

Arriving home, he saw two other students who brought the miller two old, sad nags.

"Where is your horse, Hans?" They asked.

"She will be here in three days," answered Hans.

"After three days?" - Senior students laughed.

65

"Why not in three years? What kind of horse is it that weaves slower than a person? Someone made fun of you again, you fool!" The miller, seeing Hans, became angry.

"How could you show up for my clean mill in your dirty rags?" He shouted.

"Get out!" Hans went to live in a stable. Three days later, early in the morning, a golden carriage pulled by six frisky horses rode into the mill yard. Another horse, tied behind the wagon, was prettier and more handsome than the rest. On her sat, an extraordinarily beautiful young princess.

"Miller!" She called. The miller ran out to meet her, bowing incessantly. From birth, he did not see such wealth.

"Call me your younger student, the magnificent Hans, who has been with me for seven years," the princess ordered.

"He's in a cow's style, Your Highness," said the embarrassed miller.

Servants came out of the carriage, who carried a barrel of clean water; they washed Hans and dressed him in luxurious clothes.

"Miller," said the princess, "this horse is for you from Hans."

"I have never seen such a beautiful horse," cried the joyful miller.

"The mill will rightfully go to Hans."

"Keep it all for yourself," said the princess. She put Hans in a carriage, and they sped off. Staying near the silver house built by Hans, they saw that it had turned into a magnificent castle. Hans and the princess went there. The next morning, they got married and lived their whole life happily. In the end, take a deep breath in through your nose and slowly and gently breathe out through your mouth. Again, deep breath in and gradually and breathe out one last time, deep breath in and slowly and gently breathe out. Whatever you are ready, wiggle your fingers, wriggle your toes, give a big stretch, and slowly and gently open your eyes. But remember, shine as bright as you can always.

Chapter Thirteen: Blond Princess

Close your eyes and be very still, taking a big deep breath in through your nose and slowly and gently breathe out through your mouth. Take another deep breath in and slowly and gently breathe out through your mouth. One more time, big deep breath in and slowly and gently breathe out through your mouth and relax, feeling peaceful and calm. In one big kingdom, there lived a king who had a beautiful wife. The king and queen had their only daughter, their joy, and the apple of their eye. They only dreamed about when the little princess would grow up and would give them even more pleasure. Alas, too often, dreams do not come true. The young queen died when her daughter was still very young. You cannot describe the grief that reigned at court and throughout the kingdom: after all, everyone loved the good queen. The king mourned so much that he decided never to marry again, and his only comfort and joy was a little blond princess. Some time has passed. The princess grew up and prettier every day. The king still loved her infinitely, and as soon as she wished for something, everything was fulfilled. For this, she was surrounded by a considerable entourage, and all the court ladies and servants and maids tried to warn all her desires.

Among the court ladies, there was one widow who had two red-haired daughters. She was not bad-looking herself, and her speeches were honey, but her soul was treacherous and evil. After the death of the queen, she only thought about marrying the king and making her red-haired daughters princesses. And so she began to fawn in front of a young blond princess. She lavished her praises for everything, admired her every word, and every movement. She ended all her conversations with the assurances that the blonde princess would become even happier if her father got married a second time. The young girl asked the court lady whom her father could marry.

"It is not appropriate for me to give such advice," the sly woman answered.

"God only grant that the king chooses a wife who would be kind and affectionate with our little princess. If the choice fell on me, I would only

68

think about how to be pleasant to my princess. And my daughters would be happy to serve you: while you would wash your hands, one of the daughters would hold a jug and the other a towel." The blond princess, like all children, was very gullible. She believed in the sincerity of an insidious woman, and since then, she often persuaded her father to marry her.

Finally, the daughter's persuasion worked, and the father once told her:

"I see that you will not calm down until your wish is granted. But remember: if I get married the second time, I will marry against my will and only one condition."

"What is this condition?" Asked the happy princess.

"Promise me that if you are unhappy with your new stepmother or your half-sisters, you will never complain to me and save me from troubles." The princess promised, and the king married a court lady. Some time has passed. The blonde princess turned into a beautiful girl, and the fame of her beauty spread far around. Meanwhile, her two red-haired stepsisters, on the contrary, were ugly, and their internal qualities corresponded to their external ones, so no one loved them. Young princes came from every direction from time to time and asked for the hands of the beautiful blond princess, and nobody wanted to look at the daughters of the queen. The queen held a grudge in her heart, but she showed nothing of this and was very affectionate with her stepdaughter. Among the hand seekers of the beautiful princess was the heir of the neighboring kingdom. He was very handsome and welcoming and sincerely in love with the princess. The princess was touched by his passion and fell in love with him and gave him her heart. The Queen did not like it very much since she had read one of her daughters for the prince. She took an oath to destroy both the prince and the princess and make sure that they never got married.

A convenient opportunity for this presented itself very soon. The news came that the enemy army had broken into the country, and the king went to fight. Then only the blond princess recognized her stepmother correctly. Before the king could leave, the queen showed herself in the right light. She began to treat her stepdaughter just as harshly and evilly as she had been affectionate and helpful to her shortly before. Not a day passed without

69

the stepmother scolding the young girl or the sisters. An even worse fate fell on a lot of the young prince, the groom of the princess. Once, when the prince went hunting, he got lost and fell behind his entourage. The evil queen who knew how to conjure took advantage of this. She turned the prince into a wolf and condemned him to roam the forest all his life. The prince's entourage searched for him for a long time, and when night fell, the exhausted people returned to the castle without a prince. It is hard to imagine the despair of a princess. She grieved and cried day and night, finding no solace. But the queen only laughed at her sadness and was glad that her revenge was so good at it. Once, when the blond princess was sitting alone in her room, indulging in grief, she suddenly went to that forest where the prince was lost. She asked her stepmother for permission to take a walk in the woods to disperse a little.

The queen forbade her this, but the young girl asked so fervently that she touched the heart of even this evil woman. However, the stepmother ordered one of her daughters to accompany the princess and follow her. Then both daughters argued with each other because neither of them wanted to go. Both found it boring to walk with the princess, who only did that, filled with tears. However, after much debate, the queen forced one of her daughters to go. Both young girls left the palace and were soon in the forest. The blonde princess wandered along the paths, listened to the birds singing, and thought of a friend she loved so dearly and whom she had lost forever. The sister of the princess followed her on the heels, and she was annoyed by the mournful look of the girl. After some time, they came to a small hut, hiding in dense foliage. The blond princess wanted to drink, and she asked her sister to go into the hut and ask for water.

"Enough with you and the fact that I followed you into this thicket! Is it really for me, princess, to humiliate myself even before going into some kind of dirty hut? If you want, go there alone!" The princess did not think long and entered the hut.

There on the bench sat such an old and decrepit older woman that her head shook.

"Good evening, grandmother," the princess greeted affectionately.

"Would you let me get drunk?"

"With pleasure," answered the old woman.

"Who are you? How did you get under my wretched roof?"

"I am the king's daughter," the blond princess answered, "and I went out for a walk through the forest to disperse my grief."

"What are you grieving about?" The older woman asked again.

"How can I not grieve?" - answered the princess.

"I have lost my only friend, and God alone knows if I should ever see him again." And the princess told everything to the good older woman. At this time, she cried so bitterly that she could touch the most insensitive heart. When she finished her story, the old woman told her:

"You did well to tell me your grief. I have experienced a lot in my life and am very experienced, who knows, maybe I can give you good advice. When you leave my hut, you will see a lily that has just blossomed. But this lily is not simple, it is miraculous. Hurry to rip it off. If you succeed, then do not worry about anything else: you will soon meet someone who will tell you what you should do."

After this, the princess broke up with the older woman, thanking her wholeheartedly, and the older woman remained sitting on her bench, and her head continued to shake. Meanwhile, the Queen's daughter was tired of waiting for her sister, and at the sight of her, she began to shower the princess with abuse. However, how could you expect anything else from her? The princess did not pay any attention to her and only thought about finding the lily that the older woman had told her about. They continued to walk deep into the forest. Suddenly, the princess saw a white lily not far from herself. She was delighted and rushed forward to pick a flower. But before she could run to him, he disappeared, and she saw him a few steps further from herself. The princess again rushed to the flower, but he again disappeared and appeared even further. The princess still ran after the flower, not paying attention to the fact that her sister called her. Finally, chasing a flower, she found herself at the foot of a high cliff. When she raised her head, she saw a lily at the very top of the cliff. The princess began to climb the cliff, not paying attention to either sharp stones or thorns. Finally, she climbed to the very top. This time the lily did not budge; the princess bowed, plucked it, and pressed it to her heart in delight. She was so happy that she forgot both the evil stepmother and the sisters. For a long time, the young girl sat on a cliff and could not quite admire the beautiful lily.

Suddenly she woke up and was scared at what she would say to her stepmother when she returned home so late. She began to glance around, looking for a path along which she could return to the palace. The sun was already setting, and its last rays gilded the top of the cliff on which the princess sat. Below, a dark forest blackened, and in it, it was no longer possible to distinguish a single path. The princess was desperate, but there was nothing to do: I had to spend the night on a cliff. She covered her face with her hands and wept bitterly, thinking about the evil stepmother and evil sisters and what she would have to listen to when she returned home. She also remembered her father, who was so far from her, and her friend, whom she would never have to see again. And although tears poured down her stream, she was so full of sad thoughts that she did not notice it. Twilight thickened, night fell, and stars lit up in the sky, and the princess still sat in the same place and wept bitterly, not letting go of the beautiful lily. Suddenly, a voice snapped from bitter thoughts.

"Hello, beauty! Why are you sitting here alone, and why are you so sad?"

The princess jumped up in fright, peering into the darkness, and saw a little older man who nodded affectionately to her and looked at her with sincere participation.

"How can I not be sad?" - answered the princess.

"I will never see happiness already. I have lost my darling, and now I am still lost in the forest, and I am afraid that wild animals will tear me apart."

"Don't be afraid of anything," the Old Man told her.

"If you obey me in everything, I will help you." The princess was pleased about the older man's words because she felt very lonely and abandoned by everyone. The old man handed her a flint and said:

"Now, beauty lay the fire." The princess laid out a fire of moss, dry brushwood, and dry branches and set it on fire. Flames rose to the sky itself and brightly illuminated the entire slope of the mountain.

"Now go down a little from the mountain, and you will find there a cauldron filled with resin. Bring it here."

The princess did everything as the older man ordered.

"Now put the boiler on fire!" - said the older man. The princess complied with this order. When the resin began to boil, the old man said:

"Now throw your white lily into the cauldron!" The princess was sorry to part with her lily, and she began to ask the old man to leave her a lily, but the old man told her:

"Didn't you promise to obey me in everything?"

Throw a lily in the cauldron, and there will be no harm to you! The princess turned away and threw the lily into the cauldron, although she was very sorry to part with a beautiful flower. At that moment, a dull growl was heard in the forest, which was getting closer, and, finally, the echo began to echo to him in the mountains. At the same time, a crack of dry branches and leaves was heard, and the princess saw a huge gray wolf who ran out of the forest and headed straight to the mountain on which the princess was sitting. She was terrified and would certainly have run away if the older man had not stopped her.

"Run to the edge of the cliff as soon as possible, and when the wolf finds itself under it, you pour a cauldron on it!" - said the old man.

Half-dead from fear, the princess grabbed the cauldron, rushed to the edge of the cliff, and poured tar onto the wolf as he ran under the cliff. Then a miracle happened: in an instant, the wolf threw off his wolfskin and turned into a beautiful young man who looked up at the cliff. The young girl bent down to him and only then recognized her boyfriend in this young man.

It's easy to imagine the joy of a princess! She threw up her hands and nearly fell off the cliff, but at that very moment, the prince deftly jumped onto the cliff and wrapped her in his arms. He warmly thanked her for saving him from evil spells. He did not forget to thank the good older man as well. After that, he sat on a cliff next to the princess, and they talked for a long time with each other. The prince told her that he had suffered since the evil queen turned him into a wolf, and the princess told him how she grieved and mourned her dear friend. So, they said until the morning and came to their senses only when the stars went out and the sun rose. They decided to go to the palace since paths could already be distinguished in the forest, and the wide road that led directly to the palace was visible. The cliff had a wide view, and all the surroundings lay in the palm of your hand.

"Beauty, do you see anything there? Turn around and look there."

"Yes," said the princess, "I see a rider on a soiled horse." He jumps on the road at full speed.

"This is the king's horseman," the old man replied.

"Your father returns at the head of his army."

The princess was delighted and wanted to get off the cliff as soon as possible to run towards her father. The older man stopped her and said:

"Wait! The time has not come yet. First, you need to see how it all ends." A few more minutes passed. The sun rose higher in the sky, and its rays fell on the royal palace.

"Beauty," said the old man, "turn around and see what you see there?"

"I see," said the princess, "a lot of people gathered in my father's yard. Some are sent on the road to meet the army, and others to the forest."

"These are the servants of your stepmother," said the old man. "She sent some to meet your father and others to find you in the forest." At these

74

words, the princess was frightened and wanted to run towards the queen's messengers. But the old man again restrained her and told her to wait a bit. A few more minutes passed. The young girl did not take her eyes off the road on which the king was to appear. The old man again said to her:

"Turn around, beauty, can you see anything there?"

"Yes," said the princess, "there is great excitement in my father's yard, there are a lot of people gathered there, and everyone is dressed in black."

"These are the servants of your stepmother," said the old man.

"Your stepmother wants to tell your father that you are dead."

"WHAT!" - exclaimed the princess. "Let me run out to meet my father; I want to save him from this blow."

"No," the old man answered again.

"The time has not come yet. We need to see what happens next." Meanwhile, the sun was already high, and a young girl, a beautiful young man, and an old man were still sitting motionless on a cliff. Suddenly, on the very horizon, they saw a cloud that was growing and getting closer. Soon they saw weapons and helmets sparkling, they saw banners fluttering, they heard the clang of weapons and the neighing of horses, and, finally, they distinguished the royal banner. It is difficult to describe the joy of the princess. She was eager to rush towards her father, but the old man again restrained her and said:

"Turn around, beauty! What do you see in your father's yard?"

"I see my stepmother and my sisters." They left the palace in mourning dresses. They cover their faces with white shawls and cry bitterly.

"They pretend to mourn you," said the old man.

"But wait a little longer; we have not seen everything yet."

A minute later, the old man asked again:

"Can you see something else, beautiful?"

"Yes," said the princess.

"I see that a black coffin was carried out into the yard. My father tells him to open... Ah, the queen and her daughters fell to their knees, and the king swung a sword over their heads."

"Your father wanted to see you dead," the old man explained.

"Then the evil stepmother had to tell him the whole truth."

"Now let me go," the princess exclaimed impatiently.

"Let me go and comfort the poor father."

"No," the old man answered her, "listen to me and stay here; we will see how it all ends." A few more minutes passed. Finally, the old man said again:

"Turn around, beauty. What do you see?"

"Father, stepmother, and my sisters come here, accompanied by a retinue."

"They decided to go looking for you," said the old man.

"Go down from the cliff and take the wolf skin that lies there, in the crevice of the rock." The princess complied with this order of the old man.

"And now," the old man continued, "stand on the edge of the cliff." The princess was on the edge of the cliff. Soon after, she saw a queen and her daughters under the mountain. They headed towards her.

Then the old man told her:

"Now throw the wolf skin down!" The princess threw a wolf skin, and she fell just on the queen and her daughters. A new miracle happened: barely the wolf skin touched the evil queen and her daughters when a terrible howl rang out, and they turned into wolves, which rushed to the forest with all their legs and disappeared into the thicket. Now, after this, the king appeared under the mountain with his retinue. When he raised his head and saw his daughter on a cliff, he could not believe his eyes and was petrified with amazement. Then the old man shouted:

"Now, beauty, run downstairs and make your father happy!" The princess was not forced to repeat this twice. She took the hand of her fiancé, ran away with him from the cliff, and, shedding tears of joy, rushed to her father's chest. The father and groom of the princess, and the whole retinue of the king, also cried. It was a touching sight. How much joy there was, how happy everyone was! The princess talked about what she had to endure from an evil stepmother.

The king, princess, and prince, as well as the whole retinue, went back to the palace. There the king set a great feast, at which he invited all the nobles of his kingdom. And soon, the wedding of the princess was celebrated. The feast lasted several days. And I was there. When I was driving to the wedding and driving through the forest, I met a wolf with two wolf cubs, and they all seemed fierce and gluttonous. Later I learned that they were none other than the evil stepmother and her evil daughters. In the end, take a deep breath in through your nose and slowly and gently breathe out through your mouth. Again, deep breath in and gradually and breathe out one last time, deep breath in and slowly and gently breathe out. Whatever you are ready, wiggle your fingers, wriggle your toes, give a big stretch, and slowly and gently open your eyes. But remember, shine as bright as you can always.

Chapter Fourteen: Urashima and the Tortoise

Close your eyes and be very still, taking a big deep breath in through your nose and slowly and gently breathe out through your mouth. Take another deep breath in and slowly and gently breathe out through your mouth. One more time, big deep breath in and slowly and gently breathe out through your mouth and relax, feeling peaceful and calm. Once upon a time, there lived a young fisherman who loved the sea more than anything else. He lived in a hut on the shore. In the morning and evening, winter, and summer, he did not cease to admire the sea. His name was Urashima. Every day he fished. But since he was in love with the sea and kind from nature, he always released the caught fish back into the sea. Once, throwing his fishing rod, Urashima suddenly felt that the fishing line was taut. Pulling it out, he saw a large turtle hooked on a hook. Urashima freed the turtle and released it back into the sea.

"I'd rather starve today," he thought, "than kill a young turtle."

You know that turtles live for many, many years, and this one was still very young. The turtle disappeared in the waves, and after some time of extraordinary beauty, the girl appeared at the boat of Urashima. Crouching on its edge, she said:

"I am the daughter of the sea king. We live at the bottom of the sea."

My father allowed me to turn into a tortoise to test your good heart. You are kind and noble. I invite you to visit me to see my underwater palace. Urashima could not utter a word, struck by her unearthly beauty. The only desire was to follow her everywhere.

"Yes," he could only utter, and, giving her a hand, followed her to the seabed. A crystal fish with gold fins accompanied them. Before sunset, they reached the underwater palace. It was made of coral and pearls and sparkled so that it hurt the eyes. Dragons with soft velvet skin guarded the entrance to the palace. In the silence and luxury of the palace, Urashima lived for four years with the beautiful princess. Every day, the sea sparkled and shone in the sun. They were happy until one day, Urashima met a small turtle. She reminded him of the day when he went to the sea. He remembered his village and his family. The princess knew that one day he would remember and homesick.

"You must return to earth, to the people," she said.

"If you stay here, you will hate me and die from anguish. If you go now, you can go back."

Take this pearl box tied with a green ribbon. But look, don't untie the ribbons. If you do this and open the box, you will never be able to go back. Urashima got into his boat, and the princess carried her upstairs. He swam to his native coast. Seeing him, he cried with joy. There still stood a hill, cherry trees grew, and all the same was the golden sand of the coastal sand, from which he built beautiful castles from childhood. Urashima hurried up the familiar trail. Rising, he did not recognize the surroundings. The sun also shone, birds sang and chenille, overflowing the sea. His hut was not, there was not even a tree, under whose shadow she stood. He went on. What happened in four years while he was in the underwater kingdom? Suddenly he saw a gray-haired older man resting under the shadow of a tree and went up to talk to him.

"Excuse me; you will not say how to get to the hut, Urashima?" - He asked. —

"Urashima?" - The older man asked.

"This is a very ancient name. I heard it once in my childhood. It was in the story of my great-grandfather about a boy who drowned in the sea. His brothers, their sons, and their grandchildren lived here and fished. But all of them have already died. This is an unfortunate story, right? The young man went to sea 400 years ago and did not return home. They didn't even find slivers from his boat. The sea swallowed everything," said the old man.

Without family, without a home, unfamiliar and unnecessary, Urashima was a stranger in his village. The elder, pointing towards the hill, said:

"There is a village cemetery, and there you will find his grave."

Slowly, Urashima sauntered into the cemetery. Among the names of his mother, father, and brothers, he saw his name carved on a gray gravestone. And suddenly he understood. Nothing connected him anymore with his village. Here on earth, he was dead; he was late here for 400 years. He must return to his beloved princess. He knew that he should not lose his box tied with a green ribbon. He knew he had to hurry, but he felt tired and unnecessary. He slowly returned to the shore, sat on the sea sand, and put a pearl box on his lap. He dreamed of returning to the sea kingdom. Mechanically, he untied the green ribbon and opened the box.

The white fog slowly emerged from the box and rose high into the sky. There he acquired the outlines of his beloved, lovely princess. Urashima extended his hands to her and rushed after her, but the fog cleared in the sea air. Urashima felt very old. His back hunched over in an instant, his hands shook, and his hair turned gray. His muscles became flabby, and his legs began to move barely. Soon on the seashore, children found the skeleton of an unknown person. And on the sea waves, everything swam, swinging, a small pearl box. A green ribbon circled easily in the wind above it. In the end, take a deep breath in through your nose and slowly and gently breathe out through your mouth. Again, deep breath in and gradually and breathe out one last time, deep breath in and slowly and gently breathe out. Whatever you are ready, wiggle your fingers, wriggle your toes, give a big stretch, and slowly and gently open your eyes. But remember, shine as bright as you can always.

Chapter Fifteen: Princess Cat

Close your eyes and be very still, taking a big deep breath in through your nose and slowly and gently breathe out through your mouth. Take another deep breath in and slowly and gently breathe out through your mouth. One more time, big deep breath in and slowly and gently breathe out through your mouth and relax, feeling peaceful and calm. Once the king grew old and felt that it was time to choose an heir. And he had three sons. So, he came up with a test for them. It was, however, somewhat strange. It was necessary to find the king the most devoted friend, a smart, brave, small dog. And whoever finds the smallest dog will be the king after his father. The princes were surprised, but they too honored their father to refuse this test. To each of them, his father gave a bag of gold and said:

"Meet me in a year." The brothers swore to each other to remain friends, regardless of who wins and dispersed in different directions. Each went his own way. And each of them has gone through many adventures, but I will tell only about the younger prince. He was smart, handsome, and he was always lucky in life. All that he did, he did well. And he was very brave, braver than a pack of lions. And then one evening, when the young prince made his way through the thicket in the forest, a hurricane began.

Everything was covered with darkness, and the prince got lost. Suddenly, in the distance, he saw a light and went up to him and reached the magic castle. Its doors and windows were decorated with precious stones, and the walls were made of crystal. Pictures from fairy tales were fun: about Cinderella, a little boy with a finger, Sleeping Beauty, and others painted in gold and silver. A huge diamond served as a doorknob. The prince knocked, and the door opened. Entering inside, he saw several pairs of hands holding trays of refreshments. He could not see the people, only his hands. The prince did not know what to do and stood rooted to the spot. While he was wondering if he should escape from here, one pair of hands grabbed him by the elbow and led him deep into the castle. Then, leading to the coral door, he was pushed inside. He went through sixty rooms, each of which was decorated with magical paintings. Candles in candelabra burned everywhere. Suddenly, hands appeared again from somewhere, pushed him into the middle of the sixty-first room. There was a burning fireplace and an armchair next to it. Invisible hands quickly took off his wet clothes and put on dry, even richer than his former. Then the younger prince was taken to the next room, where the walls were painted with various feline heroes. Here were the Puss in Boots, and three little kittens who lost their gloves and the cat that went to London to look at the Queen and many others. In the middle of the room stood a table with gold dishes, set for two.

A cat of extraordinary beauty with luxurious white hair entered. She was accompanied by cat servants dressed in rich clothes.

"Hello, young prince," she said. "We are glad to see you at the castle."

"Your Highness," the prince answered. "Thank you for your hospitality. You are truly the most outstanding cat I have ever seen. Your words are so courteous, and your entire palace is beyond praise."

"Young prince," said the cat. "Do not flatter me; I love simple words, ordinary people. Would you like to have lunch with me?"

Invisible hands immediately set the table and put them in dishes. A piece of mouse cake for a cat and a piece of cake with berries for a prince. The sight of the mouse pie frightened the prince, he felt uneasy, and he couldn't force himself to eat at least a piece of his food. As if guessing his thoughts, the cat said:

"Don't worry, prince, my cook is a very neat and tidy man. He knows that cats eat mice, but humans do not. Eat your food calmly."

The prince smiled and immediately ate everything. After dinner, they moved to another room. There, cats dressed in ballroom costumes began to entertain them with Spanish and Chinese dances. After this, the prince was taken to the bedroom and put to bed. The walls in the bedroom were decorated with paintings of various colors made from the wings of moths and bird feathers. The next day, early in the pre-lunch, the sound of the trumpet woke the prince.

The hands of an invisible servant handed clothes for hunting, and he went downstairs, where a magic wooden horse was waiting for him, who ran and rode no worse than the real one. The cat princess herself was riding on a hunt on a monkey. After the hunt, at dinner, the prince was presented with a magic drink, after drinking, which he immediately forgot who he was and where he came from, and why he had come here. He only wanted to be constantly in the company of the charming Cat Princess. They went hunting, fish, read, and played the piano. They listened to cat operas and watched cat ballet, and all this time, they were served by the hands of an invisible, tireless servant. And then, one day, the Princess Cat said to the prince:

"Three days later, you must return to your father and bring him a small dog."

"Oh, my God!" Cried the prince. "How could I forget about that?! But how do I manage to get a dog, buy a horse, and get home? And all this in three days..." The princess cat mysteriously smiled:

"Prince, you are my friend. And I will help you. My magical, wooden horse will take you home in twenty-four hours."

"What about the dog?" The prince asked.

"There she is," the princess answered, and gave him a small seed.

"Put it in your ear," she ordered. He did so, and the grain in his ear suddenly barked so-and-so.

"Do not open this seed until you return to your father," she said. The prince returned home before the brothers, but they soon came. The king appeared before his sons. The younger prince handed him a seed.

"This is your father," he said. The king opened the seed. A tiny dog jumped out of its center covered in velvet, which was smaller than a hole for a mace head. She bowed sweetly and danced a Spanish dance for the king. The king was very happy but decided to give his sons one more test.

"Now," he said. "Bring me each a dress that would fit into the eye of a needle. I give you one year." The princess went in different directions, and the youngest went straight to the cat's palace! The princess was very glad to see him and, after listening to his story, she said:

"Do not worry, live calmly, I will arrange everything in the best way." So another year passed. One day, the princess, waking the prince early in the morning, said:

"Tomorrow you must return to your father. And bring him a dress. The horse carriage is ready. Hit the road."

"Here is a walnut for your father. Opening it, he will find in it what he wanted."

"My dear princess," said the prince. "I feel so good with you that I really don't want to go back to my father. I don't need a royal throne; I want to be near you." The cat smiled and said:

"You have to come back. Father is waiting for you."

The prince has returned home. The brothers were already in the palace. The dresses brought were by far the finest beautiful. But when the king tried to stretch his clothes through the eye of a needle, nothing came of it. Then the young prince stepped forward. He handed the walnut to the king. Everyone smiled and thought it was just a joke. The king discovered the nut, there was a bean grain inside. He dug up grain and discovered wheat grain. The prince was worried. But when the king discovered this grain and took out a lovely royal dress from it, everyone was dumbfounded! It shimmered and sparkled with all the colors of the rainbow. It depicted the most outlandish animals, birds, fish, everything, everything, everything in the world! It freely passed through the eye of the needle.

"I am very glad," said the king. "And now I give you the last task: Bring me the most beautiful of the girls who will become your bride. I'll meet you in a year."

The prince hit the road, and the youngest went straight to the cat's palace.

"I already know everything," said the Cat Princess. "I will help you."

The third year sped even faster than the first two. The prince and the princess cat hunted, played chess, read aloud fairy tales. Finally, the day came home.

"Now, all your happiness is in your hands," said the cat.

"I am a bewitched princess, and you can bewitch me."

"But how?!" - Cried out the prince.

"Cut off my head and tail and burn them in the fire," said the cat.

"Cut off your head? Never! You are dearer to me than hundreds of crowns and thrones. Not a single hair will fall from your head."

"You have to do this," the cat insisted.

"You and I will only get better from this." The prince's heart was filled with anxiety. But he agreed... Although his hands trembled violently, the young man did everything the cat ordered. And then a miracle happened, in front of him stood a girl of such unearthly beauty that anyone who ever saw her at once would immediately fall in love with her without memory, forgetting about everything in the world. Immediately, all the cat-servants turned into people. And the princess told the prince her story.

"I was not always a cat," she said. "My father owned six kingdoms, and my mother loved traveling." Once, she heard a story about an outlandish fruit growing in an old, abandoned castle. And immediately went there.

But the castle gates were tightly closed from the inside, and the walls were so high and impregnable that there was no way to get there. The queen fell ill from the disease, realizing that she would not be able to taste the strange fruit. And then one day an old woman suddenly appeared in front of her.

"Queen," she said. "I know you want to taste the strange fruit so badly that you die without it. I agree to bring it, but in return, you must give me your daughter, whom you will soon give birth."

The Queen, distraught with curiosity, agreed.

"I will endow your daughter with kindness, wisdom, beauty, and nobility, but you should not see her until she is twenty years old. You take a stern promise from me. But I agree," the queen said, the maid dressed her and led her into the garden, where there was a strange tree with fruits. The queen tasted the fruit, and the old woman pulled her another whole basket and gave her with her. Soon after, I was born. My mother was afraid of her promise. She could not tell her father about this and soon fell into deep anguish.

My father was very worried and, through long interrogations, got the truth from her. He was beside himself with rage. He ordered his wife to be locked up in jail, and her daughter strenuously guarded. The fairies became angry with the king and sent to his kingdom all the worst diseases in the world. Every day, hundreds of children, old people, and women died. Terrified, the king turned to a wizard friend and asked for his help.

"I can do nothing," said the wizard.

"The word needs to be kept!" My father reconciled; he released my mother from prison. She put me in a golden cradle and carried me to the fairies. They gladly accepted me and carried me to the fortress which they built especially for me. There were many lovely rooms, and the roof was a blooming garden. There were no doors in the fortress; there were only very high windows. Several years have passed there. And the fairies decided it was time for me to get married. They chose King Tinney as my husband.

On the eve of the wedding, my friend, a parrot, flew to me and said.

"Poor princess, my little one. I'm so sorry for you."

"Why?" I asked.

"Because your future husband, King Tinney, is a terrible freak and monster. He lives on the same tree like me." Before he had time to say this, one of the fairies came in and said:

"Get ready and get down quickly. King Tinney came there, be more pleasant with him."

"But I don't want to see him and marry him," I cried...

"Silly child! I know better who you need as a husband. Just dare to disobey me."

I went downstairs in tears and saw him. He was no bigger than a parrot. He had the clawed legs of an eagle, the hump, and the ugly face of an evil dwarf. His nose was sharp, long as a pencil. He wanted to kiss me, but I ran away in horror and shut myself in my room. Then the cruel fairies enchanted my servants and me turning us all into cats and cats. Witchcraft was supposed to end only when a young prince appeared in my palace who would love me.

"I love you more than life," said the prince. "And I want to marry you." They went to the palace. And the princess hid inside a ruby testicle. The brothers of the prince were already in the palace.

Both with beautiful princesses. When the turn came to the youngest, he opened a ruby testicle and a princess emerged from it, overshadowing day and night, the sun and moon. She was dressed in pink and white clothes, and her head was decorated with a wreath of outlandish flowers.

"Yes!" - Shouted the joyful king.

"Only she is worthy of my palace!"

"Your Majesty," the princess answered. "Thank you for your trust. But I do not need your palace. I have six of them! Let me give two of them to your eldest sons? And to marry the youngest and settle in the remaining four palaces."

Everyone was happy, and immediately, the priest married three young couples who happily lived the rest of their lives. In the end, take a deep breath in through your nose and slowly and gently breathe out through your mouth. Again, deep breath in and gradually and breathe out one last time, deep breath in and slowly and gently breathe out. Whatever you are ready, wiggle your fingers, wriggle your toes, give a big stretch, and slowly and gently open your eyes. But remember, shine as bright as you can always.

Chapter Sixteen: Grace and Derek

Close your eyes and be very still, taking a big deep breath in through your nose and slowly and gently breathe out through your mouth. Take another deep breath in and slowly and gently breathe out through your mouth. One more time, big deep breath in and slowly and gently breathe out through your mouth and relax, feeling peaceful and calm. Once upon a time, there was a king with a queen, and they had an only daughter, whose name was Grace. This name was very suitable for her. She was beautiful, kind, and smart. Grace was the decoration of the palace, and many royal advisers asked her for advice before making decisions. In the mornings, her mother taught her the art of being a queen. The servants served her a table with silver and gold appliances and served the most luxurious and exotic dishes in the world; in a word, she was the happiest of girls. Among the ladies of the palace was the ever-dissatisfied and envious Duchess of Gruge; she had greasy hair and a round red face. She was a slut, a sloth, and, besides, one of her legs was shorter than the other.

She hated Grace, who was getting prettier and prettier every day. Once the queen fell ill and died. Grace was very homesick for his mother, and the king inconsolably mourned the death of his wife. So, a year has passed. The king was sick and tired of longing, and the doctors told him more often to be in the fresh air. The king decided to go hunting. One fine day, having gone on a hunt, he stopped to rest in a large mansion. It was the home of the Duchess of Gruge. She went out to meet the king and escorted him to the cool part of the house, where he lay down to rest. After a hearty dinner, the duchess led the king to show her wine cellars.

"Let me offer you some old wine," she said.

"What kind of wine are stored here?" The king asked.

"We'll see now," the duchess replied. She pulled the cork from one barrel. Thousands of gold coins fell to the floor.

"How strange," said the duchess. She pulled the cork from another barrel, and tens of thousands of coins fell from a new barrel.

"Still, this is very strange," the duchess grinned. And she began to pull out corks from each barrel in a row. Pearls and diamonds, sapphires, and emeralds sprinkled on the cellar floor.

"Oh, Your Highness, there seems to be no fault at all." Instead, the barrels are full of some trash, said the sly duchess.

"Junk?" Cried the astonished king.

"Do you call wealth trash?"

"You have not seen my wealth yet," said Grace, who simply reveled in her cunning. "All my cellars are full of gold and precious stones." All of them will be yours if you marry me.

"My dear Duchess, of course, I will marry you!" - exclaimed the king, who simply adored the money.

"But I have one condition," said Grace. "I want to be the guardian of your daughter, and I insist that she obey me implicitly."

"Good," the king agreed. The duchess handed him the keys to the cellars, and on the same day, they got married in a small church. Arriving home, the king immediately went to his daughter's room.

"Well, how was the hunt?" Grace asked. "Is the booty great?"

"The tremendous booty is the countless treasures of the Duchess of Grace, whom we married this morning. Now you have to love her, respect, and obey unquestioningly. Go change into your best clothes. Today I will bring the duchess to the palace."

Grace loved her father very much and just wanted him to be happy, but she could not keep the flood of tears. Her nanny saw this, asking what happened.

"My father married again," Grace sobbed. "And my stepmother is my archenemy, the Duchess of Gruge."

"Never forget that you are a princess, dear. Be able to hide your feelings. Promise me that the duchess will never know about your attitude to her," the old nanny asked. It was very hard. But Grace promised herself to meet the Duchess with a happy face and very good intentions. She wore a young green dress and a gold robe. Grace also did a beautiful hairstyle and crowned her with a crown studded with diamonds.

Grace also prepared herself carefully for the meeting. She put on a high-heeled shoe on her short leg, dyed her hair black, and her face was powdered richly. And the dressmaker sewed her a dress hiding the hump. Sending a walker with a note to the king, she wrote that she would like to enter the royal court on the king's most beautiful horse. While preparations were underway, Grace went out for a walk in the forest. Here no one bothered to cry ad libitum. Calming down, she looked up and saw a charming little page dressed in a green silk camisole and a white velvet hat. He was smiling, approaching her.

"Princess, the king is waiting for you." Grace was puzzled.

"Why did she never see him among the royal servants?"

"How long have you been serving with us? She asked.

"I do not serve any king, my dear. I serve only you. My name is Derek. I am the prince of the magic kingdom. At birth, I was endowed with magical powers that allowed me to be with you wherever you are, remaining invisible. I heard all your conversation with your father and came to help you."

"So, you are the very clever prince in the world, Derek, whom I heard so much about. I am glad that you offer me your help. Now I'm not so afraid of the Duchess of Gruge," said Grace.

They returned to the castle. Derek chose the most beautiful horse for the princess, and she and her father left to meet the duchess. In the turmoil of preparations, no one noticed that Grace's horse is a hundred times more beautiful than the horse chosen for the duchess. The duchess's motorcade met them halfway. The king helped the duchess get out of the carriage and escorted her to the horse of her choice. Seeing Grace's horse, the ugly duchess screamed in a terrible voice:

"What a mockery this is! Why is this girl a better horse than mine? I refuse to go to the castle and return home."

The king began to beg the duchess not to do this and ordered Grace to give her his horse to her. Climbing into the saddle, the Duchess angrily whipped the horse so that it flew faster than the whirlwind. And no matter how Gruge tried to stay in the saddle, she still fell into a muddy puddle. The king ran to her, picked him up, and carried her to the palace, where the servants put her to bed.

"It was Grace who set me up," the evil duchess yelled, "She did it to humiliate me. She wanted to kill me!"

The king decided to appease Gruge. He knew how she wanted to be beautiful and ordered for her a portrait that royal painters could have embellished. He gave a ball in honor of the Duchess and put her in the most honorable place. The Duchess shone with happiness. It seemed to her that everyone was just doing what they were looking at her. In fact, all the invited princes, kings, dukes, and barons looked at Grace, who was standing behind her stepmother. Seeing this, the duchess decided to destroy her stepdaughter.

Late at night, the guard grabbed Grace and drove away into a forest full of wild animals. There she was left alone. Wandering through the wild, dark forest, Grace cried, wailing...

"Oh, Derek, where are you? Did you really leave me?"

And suddenly, a miracle happened. A candle was lit on each branch of each tree, illuminating the road to a magnificent crystal palace, standing in the depths of the forest. Walking closer to him, she saw on the threshold of a radiant Derek, who held out his hands to her.

"Don't be afraid, my dear, because I love you so much," he said.

"We're going to the palace; my mother and sisters were waiting for you." Wonderful music played everywhere in the palace. The Queen and her daughters led Grace into a magical crystal room, where the astonished princess saw in the mirrors her whole life and all the adventures that had happened to her.

"I want to remember everything about you forever," Derek explained. Grace did not know what to say. Then the queen intervened and called everyone to the table. After a hearty dinner, Grace felt tired.

Thirty handmaids stripped her and put her to bed, where she sweetly fell asleep to the quiet, melodious music. When she woke up, they showed her cabinets full of dresses and jewelry, as well as many beautiful shoes. Everything was her size and her taste. Grace thanked Derek for all this.

"I have to go," she said. "My father must be worried."

"You're safe here," Derek objected to her. "Why would you leave? Marry me and forget your past, like a bad dream. We will live well here."

"I would love to stay here," Grace replied. "But my duty is now to be with my father, who will go crazy, deciding that I have died. In addition, I am very afraid that this nasty Gruge will plague him to death."

Derek tried to persuade Grace, but it was all useless. In the end, he agreed to let her go. He made her invisible so that she could quietly get into the castle. Grace, penetrating the castle, immediately went to her father's room. At first, he was very scared, taking Grace for a ghost, but then he calmed down and listened to her. She explained to her father that Gruge wanted to kill her, and only by a miracle, she managed to escape. She asked her father to send her to the farthest end of the kingdom so that she could live there calmly without Grudge intrigues.

The king, although he was a bold and strong-willed man, was under the heel of his new wife. He reassured Grace and invited her to dinner with him. The servants of the duchess saw Grace and reported to her that the princess had returned unharmed to the palace. When the king fell asleep, the duchess began to act. She grabbed Grace, dressed her in tattered rags, and put her in a prison pit. Instead of a bed, she threw a bundle of straw there. Grace was very homesick for her native palace, sweet father, and good Derek. But nobody called for help. At that time, Gruge and his girlfriend, an evil fairy, thought up the most terrible punishments for Grace. Finally, the fairy, straining her mind sophisticated in filth, said:

"Let's try this." They gave her a bewitched ball of tangled threads and told her to take it apart and rewind it until morning. No matter how hard Grace tried, the fur only became more tangled and tangled. Grace set the ball aside and burst into tears.

"Better Gruge kill me than suffer so much," she sobbed.

"Oh, Derek, if you can't help me, then at least come and say goodbye to me." Before she could utter the last words, out of nowhere, Prince Derek appeared.

"Don't cry, my dear," he said. "Come with me; we will get married and live happily."

"But how can I verify that you really love me, we have known each other for a very short time." - Said Grace.

Derek only sadly bowed his head to hide his tears and, saying goodbye to her, disappeared. Gruge could hardly wait for the night, anticipating reprisal against Grace. She brought Grace a huge bag full of various bird feathers and demanded that Grace separate them by species. The feathers were so colorful and different, and there were so many that it was simply an impossible task. No one could, except for the birds themselves, distinguish which feather belongs to which species.

"I won't call Derek anymore," Grace thought. "If he really loves me, he will come here himself."

"I'm here, my dear!" - A voice was heard from above, and she saw her beloved. He waved his wand three times, and all the feathers themselves were divided into the necessary heaps.

"How grateful I am to you for everything," Grace warmly thanked him.

"I will never forget your kindness to me!" The next morning, seeing that all the work was done correctly and on time, Grudge came into an indescribable rage. She rushed to her friend, a sorceress, and begged her to give Grace the most impossible job.

"Take this magic box," said the evil fairy.

"If Grace opens it, it will never close. Send her with her and strictly punish her not to open it, curiosity will prevail anyway, and Grace will open the box. Then you will have a reason to punish her."

Gruge followed the sorceress's order exactly and, giving Grace a box, said:

"Take it to me on the estate. Yes, look, do not look into it, because there are things that are too expensive for you to see them. I forbid you this under pain of death." Grace took the box and hit the road. Having walked almost half the way, she stopped to rest. Crouching on the grass, she laid the box on her knees and thought:

"I wonder what's inside. I will open it once and will not touch anything." She opened the box, and from there suddenly, a whole flock of tiny transparent little men flew out, the largest of which was with the nail of a human little finger. They whirled a little in the air and disappeared.

"Oh God, what have I done," Grace cried. "Because of my curiosity, I was in trouble. Oh Derek, if you still love me, so stupid, help me soon!"

The prince appeared immediately. He waved his wand and tiny little men, suddenly flocking from all sides, immediately jumped into the box and closed the lid behind him. Once again, he waved his wand, and his carriage appeared. Derek put Grace in her and drove her to the Gruge estate. But the servants did not let Grace in, as she was in dirty rags. The princess was forced to go back to the palace. By the time she returned, the evil duchess had matured a new plan. In the garden, she ordered a large pit to be dug with a trap at the bottom and grass laid on top of it. In the evening, together with her maids and Grace, she went for a walk in the garden. Passing by the pit, she pushed the poor princess there, and she, with the maidservants, fled back to the palace. Poor Grace cried bitterly in a dark, damp pit.

"I'm buried here alive," she sobbed.

"Oh, Derek, here's the punishment for me not believing your love." Suddenly she heard a strange rustling and, turning around, saw that a door appeared in one of the corners of the pit, which began to increase and increase.

Light shone through her. Opening it, Grace saw a blooming garden with outlandish flowers and fruits and a fountain of extraordinary beauty. And ahead was the huge crystal palace of Prince Derek. The prince himself, his mother and sisters went out to meet her.

"Dear prince," said Grace. "I did not believe your love, but you proved it to me. If you don't change your mind, I'll be happy to marry you."

They immediately got married and lived happily in the magical kingdom, where they still live. In the end, take a deep breath in through your nose and slowly and gently breathe out through your mouth. Again, deep breath in and gradually and breathe out one last time, deep breath in and slowly and gently breathe out. Whatever you are ready, wiggle your fingers, wriggle your toes, give a big stretch, and slowly and gently open your eyes. But remember, shine as bright as you can always.

Chapter Seventeen: Green Snake

Close your eyes and be very still, taking a big deep breath in through your nose and slowly and gently breathe out through your mouth. Take another deep breath in and slowly and gently breathe out through your mouth. One more time, big deep breath in and slowly and gently breathe out through your mouth and relax, feeling peaceful and calm. Once upon a time, there was a queen, in whom twin daughters were born once. She called to the christening fairies. And in those days, if fairies came to baptize a child, they brought him many gifts as a gift. They could turn an ordinary child into the most beautiful and smartest in the world. But sometimes the fairies, angry at something, could wish the baby a lot of bad things, so all the parents tried to appease the fairies. And in the palace was arranged a magnificent banquet for fairies. Before the fairies could start eating, an old, old fairy appeared that had not been seen for many years. The Queen shook in horror from a terrible foreboding. And the king, running to the old woman, wanted to seat her at the table, but she rudely pushed him away and said:

"I do not need your handouts."

"Well, please," the queen pleaded, "honor us with seeing you at our table."

"If you wanted this, you would invite me," the ugly old woman exclaimed indignantly.

"If you think that the power of my magic has decreased over the years, then this is not so, and soon I will prove it to you." Finally, she deigned to sit at the table, but her anger began to boil with renewed vigor when she saw the belts dotted with precious stones that other fairies received as gifts from the king and queen. She did not get a belt. The frightened queen brought her a box decorated with diamonds, but the old hag pushed the gift away, saying indignantly:

"Here is another proof that you did not even think of inviting me. Take away your box, and I have so many diamonds that you have never dreamed of!" She struck the table twice with a magic wand, and instead of sumptuous

98

dishes, ugly wriggling snakes appeared on the dishes. In horror, all the fairies fled. As soon as they disappeared, the old hag approached the first child's crib and said:

"I wish you to be as disgusting and terrible as possible." She already approached another crib, but here she didn't! A young, bold fairy jumped up, remaining in the throne room, and grabbed her by the back. The old hag burst out of anger and burned.

The returning fairies tried to reward the poor injured baby with her best gifts. But the queen was inconsolable, seeing that from every moment, her daughter was becoming uglier and uglier.

"How can we help her?" - argued fairies. They consulted a little.

"Your Majesty," they said, "do not cry. We promise you that one day your daughter will become the happiest girl in the world."

"And will she be beautiful?" Asked the inconsolable queen.

"We cannot explain everything," the fairies answered.

"But believe us, she will be happy." The queen thanked them and gave them rich gifts. She named the first daughter Dagley, and the second, Dorabella. Dagley became more and more terrible over the years, and Dorabella became more beautiful and more beautiful. When Dagley turned 12, she became so terrible that no one could even approach her without disgust. Therefore, the king bought the most remote castle in the kingdom and put her there to live alone. She went there with her old nanny and several servants. The old castle stood on the seashore. On the other hand, there was a dense forest, beyond which vast fields stretched. Dagley lived there for two long years. She studied music and painting and even composed a whole book of poems. But she missed her parents and once decided to visit them. Doral arrived just at the time when her sister was marrying a prince from a neighboring kingdom. Relatives were not at all pleased with her. They were unpleasant to look at her ugliness, and they were afraid that the prince, seeing her, would refuse to marry her sister, Dorabella. Poor Dagley, through tears, said to them:

"I came only to see you for a minute. I missed you so much! But you do not want to see me, and I'm leaving right away!"

She wanted to remind them that her ugliness was not her fault, but theirs. But she had a very kind heart, and she did not begin to do this, but only in tears left the palace. Once, while walking through the woods, she saw a huge green snake, which, raising its head, said to her in a human voice:

"Good morning, Dagley. Do not be sad. Look at me. I'm much uglier than you. And once I was attractive."

Doral was very scared and ran home. For several days she was afraid to leave the house, but one evening, tired of the monotony of the palace rooms, she went for a walk to the sea. Going to the shore, she saw a luxurious little golden boat, all strewn with precious stones and shining in the rays of the setting sun. Her oars were made of pure gold.

The boat slowly swayed on the waves, and Dagley went to see her closer. She entered the boat and went down into a small cabin, sheathed in green velvet. While she was considering the decoration of the cabin, the wind blew, and the boat quickly sailed into the open sea. Doral first tried to stop the boat, but then thought:

"I will surely die, and then my torment will come to an end. I'm so ugly that everyone hates me. My sister became the queen, and I'm a terrible ugly. Only ugly snakes want to talk to me."

Suddenly, among the waves appeared a green snake which said in a human voice:

"Died, if you do not reject the help of an ugly snake, I can save your life."

"Better I die," Dagley said, as she had been afraid of snakes. Without a word, the snake disappeared into the waves.

"This green reptile terrifies me. I just shake with fear when I see these eyes burning with yellow fire and the sting sticking out of a disgusting mouth. I'd rather die than trust her with my life. But why is she chasing me? And how

100

did she learn to speak?" Dagley thought. Suddenly, the wind conveyed to hear the words:

"Princess, be affectionate with a green snake. In the end, she is wonderful for a snake, unlike you. She can help you, even in that which you do not assume. Let her do it."

A hurricane flew over, drove the boat into the reefs, and, breaking it to smithereens, subsided. Doral grabbed a piece of the boat, barely fitting on it. Suddenly she was horrified to find that she was not holding on to a piece of wood but on the body of a green snake. After some time, they swam to the rock, and the snake, having landed Dagley ashore, disappeared again. Dagley, sitting alone on a rock, cried, saying:

"I escaped from the storm, but here I am sure to die." The evening was approaching. Climbing to the clifftop, Dagley lay down, covered in an apron, and fell asleep. In a dream, she heard the most wonderful music she had ever heard. What a wonderful dream, Dagley thought, and reaching out, opened her eyes. But what was her surprise when she suddenly saw not a sea around herself and not a rock underneath, but a beautiful golden hall with a gilded balcony. Entering the balcony, Dagley saw blooming gardens and forests, a huge old park with sparkling fountains and statues of extraordinary work. In the distance, shimmering with all the rainbow colors, there were small houses strewn with precious stones.

"What is it with me? Where am I?" - Dagley was perplexed.

Suddenly she heard a knock on the door. Going up and opening it, she found on the threshold of fifty small Chinese dolls, alive, like ordinary people. They were the size of a hand, but they laughed and spoke like people. They greeted Dagley and expressed the hope that she would like in their wonderful kingdom.

"Our dear guest," said the smallest doll, which was the main one among them.

"Our dear king wished us to make your presence here very happy. Therefore, we are at your disposal."

They led Dagley to the garden, where they showed her a luxurious pool. Near the pool, she saw two large chairs.

"Whose is it?" She asked.

"One king," said the dolls, "and the second is yours."

"But, where is the king?"

"I don't see him," said Dagley.

"He's fighting in the war now," the chrysalis answered.

"Is he married?" Dagley asked.

"No," the doll answered.

"He has not yet met his dream." Having bathed in the pool, Dagley put on the luxurious clothes that the dolls brought her. They combed her hair and decorated her hair with precious stones. Dagley was happy. For the first time in her life, she felt like a princess. A week passed unnoticed. Dagley was happy, dolls too. They fell in love with her for a kind heart.

One night, lying in her bed, she wondered what would happen next. For some reason, she felt lonely anyway.

"This is because you do not know love," a voice from above answered her thoughts.

"Real happiness comes only to loving people."

"Which of the pupae is talking to me?" Dagley asked.

"This is not a doll. It's me, the king of all these lands, my dear. And I love you with all my heart."

"Does the prince love me?" Asked the startled Dagley.

"You must be blind. I'm the scariest freak in the world."

"No, I see you very well, and once again, I dare to say that you are the most beautiful girl in the world."

"You are very kind," said Dagley.

"I don't even know what to say." The invisible king said nothing more that night. The next day, Dagley asked the pupae if the king had returned home, and their answer:

"Not yet," very puzzled her.

"Is he young and handsome?" She asked.

"Yes, and he is also very kind. He tells us news about himself every day."

"But does he know that I'm here?" She asked.

"Yes, he knows everything about you."

Every hour, walkers deliver him a detailed report of your stay here. Since then, barely feeling lonely, Dagley heard the voice of the invisible king. He always said nice and kind words to her. One night, waking up, she saw a foggy figure next to her bed. She thought that this was one of the dolls guarding her sleep, and held out her hand, trying to touch the figure. Suddenly, someone began to kiss her hand, and a few drops of tears spilled on her. Dagley suddenly realized that this was an invisible king.

"What do you want from me?" She asked.

"How can I love you if I have never seen your face?"

"My beloved princess," answered the invisible king, "The fact is that I cannot show you my face. The wicked old sorceress who has brutally treated you has cast a seven-year spell on me. Five years have passed, only two years left. And if you now agree to marry me, they will be the happiest in my life."

Touched by the kindness and nobility of the invisible king, Dagley immediately fell in love with him and agreed to marry him. However, she promised that she would not insist on seeing him for the remaining two years of the spell.

"The thing is, my beloved," said the invisible king, "that if you break your vow, then from that moment, the seven years of the spell will begin again. And if you keep your promise, then in two years I will appear before you the most beautiful man in the world, and you will also become the most beautiful of the queens, since your beauty, selected by the evil sorceress, will return to you."

Dagley promised him to be patient and inquisitive, and soon they got married. A few months after the wedding, Dagley was very homesick for her relatives. She asked the king to allow her to invite them to visit. The invisible king tried to dissuade her, but everything was in vain. Finally, he allowed her to send dolls to her family across the sea with an invitation to visit their palace. Mother Dagley was very interested to see her son-in-law. She immediately hit the road, taking Dorabella with her. Dagley, with great pleasure, showed them her palace. When they were interested in her husband, she lied to them, as she could, saying that he was in the war, now on the hunt, then just sick.

But since she was a very truthful girl, she did not know how to lie, and mother and sister decided that she had no husband at all. They began to pry out the truth from her. Unable to withstand their inquiries, Dagley told them the whole truth.

"He's just making a fool of you," the mother and sister told her after listening to her story.

"Do you really believe his words? Or maybe he is a terrible monster who wants to kill you?"

Mother's words terribly bothered Dagley. After seeing her home with rich gifts, Dagley decided to find out the secret of her invisible husband to the end. One night, she put a lamp near her bed, and when the king approached her bed, she lit his face. Oh, God! It was not a king, but a huge green snake.

"Oh, my God!" Cried the king, bursting into tears.

"Why did you punish me so much, because I love you more than life!" Dagley, in response, only silently shook with fear. The green snake has disappeared. In the morning, the dolls appeared very sad, because they had just received news that the evil sorceress sent enemies to their kingdom puppets.

The dolls fought bravely and defeated them. Then the sorceress whirled a whirlwind of dust and dirt throughout the kingdom of the invisible king. Only Dagley survived. Puppets captured her and led her to the old sorceress.

"Hello, dear," said the old woman.

"It seems to me that we met before with you." She laughed.

"I once walked perfectly on your christening."

"Really," Dagley pleaded, "then you didn't punish me enough by making you a hideous ugly? Why are you still hurting me now by doing this to my husband?"

"You talk too much," said the old woman.

"Hey, servants, bring the iron shoes and put them on the queen." Servants pulled narrow and heavy shoes on the queen. Then the old hag gave her a terrible spindle, pricking fingers to the blood and a tangled ball of web.

"Unravel it for two hours and hide it in beautiful yarn."

"I cannot spin, but I will try," Dagley replied. She was taken to a dark, pretentious little closet and locked. Dagley tried several times to unravel the web, but she did not succeed. She stabbed her fingers to the blood.

Dropping her head on her chest, she wept bitterly, remembering her serene, happy life in the palace, which she had lost due to her own stupidity. Suddenly she heard a familiar voice.

"My beloved, why did you make me suffer so much? But I love you and want you to be saved. I have one friend left."

"Fairy Patroness and I asked her to help you."

Suddenly, someone clapped his hands three times, and Dagley's web turned into a pretty yarn. Two hours later, a sorceress appeared, anticipating reprisal.

"Well, you didn't strain, ugly sloth," she yelled from the threshold.

"I did everything I could," Dagley answered, handing her a skein of beautiful yarn.

"You think you can outwit me," the witch shook with anger, "Well, then, my second task. Weave a net from this yarn, so strong that it can catch salmon."

"But, grandmother," Dagley answered her, "even flies sometimes break the net from the web."

"I will destroy you if you do not complete my task," the old woman hissed viciously. As soon as she left, Dagley wept bitterly and, raising her hands to the sky, said:

"Fairy Patroness, I beg you, help me." Before she could finish, the network was ready. Dagley thanked the fairy and added:

"My beloved king! Only now I realized how I did not appreciate your love and caused you so much suffering. Forgive me if you can." When the witch saw the net, she was furious.

"I will take you to my palace, and no one will be able to help you there," she cried. She grabbed Dagley and ordered the servants to take her on a ship to her state. At night, sitting on the deck, Dagley looked at the stars and mourned her fate. Suddenly she heard a familiar voice.

"Don't worry, my love. I will save you." Dagley looked at the water and saw a green snake. Suddenly, out of nowhere, an evil sorceress appeared. She never slept and heard the voice of the invisible king.

"A green snake," she cried in a terrible voice, "I order you to sail away from here to the very end of the world and not appear here again. You, Dagley, will see what I will do with you when we arrive at the place."

The green snake sailed to the place of its detention. The Natures ship arrived at the scene. The sorceress took Dagley, tied a huge stone to her neck, and gave her a bucket full of holes.

"Climb the cliff," she ordered her. "At the top of the cliff is a wild forest full of evil beasts guarded by the Well of Wisdom and Patience. Go there and brought me a bucket full of water from this well. And hurry up, I give you three years to do this."

"But how can I climb this rock?" Dagley pleaded.

"How can I bring water in a holey bucket?"

"I don't care how you do it," the witch burst out laughing, "do it, or I will kill the green snake," Dagley promised herself that the green snake will never suffer because of her, and she set to work. Fairy Patroness helped her.

A strong wind rose Dagley to the top of the cliff. Fairy tamed wild animals with her magic wand. After another wave of a magic wand, a chariot drawn by two eagles appeared. Dagley warmly thanked the fairy, but she smiled and said:

"The green snake asked me to help you." Eagles instantly take you to the Well of Wisdom and Patience. They will also fill your bucket with water. When you receive the water of Wisdom and Patience, wash your face with it, and your beauty will return to you.

"How wonderful!" - exclaimed Dagley.

"But you have to hurry up and do what I tell you before returning to the witch. Your spell has made you a slave for exactly seven years. Birds will take you to the forest. Pass the term of your spell there." Dagley warmly thanked the fairy and said:

"All your gifts and even the beauty that should come back to me will not bring me satisfaction. I cannot be happy while the green snake suffers."

"If you are brave all the remaining years of your spell, you will be free and the green snake too," the fairy promised.

"Is it really such a long time I will not see and hear him?" Dagley asked.

"Unfortunately, no," the fairy answered.

"Your spell does not allow you to receive news from him." Tears spilled from Dagley's eyes at these words. She sat in a chariot, and the eagles rushed her to the Well of Wisdom and Patience. When the eagles filled her bucket with water so that not a drop spilled, Dagley thought:

"This water can make me wiser. I'll probably take a sip and become smarter. And then I'll wash myself to be beautiful." She first drank a sip of magic water. Then she washed her face. She became so attractive that all the birds around immediately sang, looking at her beauty. A good fairy appeared at once and said:

"Your desire to become wiser than more beautiful makes me happy. And I will cut your spell by three years."

"Thank you," said Dagley.

"But instead, better help the green snake."

"I'll try," the fairy said.

"But look at yourself. How beautiful you have become; you cannot be called more Dagley. I gave you a new name, 'Queen of Discretion.'" Before disappearing, the fairy touched the queen's feet, and the tight ugly iron shoes turned into a pair of gold slippers.

Birds rushed the Queen of Discretion into the forest. How beautiful it was there. Birds of paradise sang in the trees of paradise, and the animals around spoke in human voices.

"The fairy sent us a guest," the eagles informed everyone around.

"This is the Queen of Discretion."

"Oh, how beautiful she is!" - The animals rustled,

"Please become our mistress!"

"With pleasure," Discretion said, "But tell me first, what is this place where we are now?" The wise old mole answered her:

"Many, many years ago, fairies were tired of fighting human laziness, lies, and idleness. At first, they tried to reason people but then became angry with them and turned boors into pigs, chatty gossips became parrots or hens, and liars became monkeys. This forest has become their home. They will be here until the fairies consider that they are sufficiently trained."

The animals are very fond of the good, wise, beautiful Discretion. They collected nuts for her, fed her berries, and entertained with fairy tales. Truly, anyone would be happy in this paradise. But Discretion was constantly tormented by thoughts of what misfortune she brought to the green snake. Three years quickly flew by. The Queen of Discretion again put on her iron shoes, took a bucket of water of wisdom, put a chain with a stone on her neck, and asked the eagles to send her to the old sorceress.

The old hag was very surprised to see her. She believed that Discretion had long died, or that wild animals in the forest had torn her to pieces. But now, in front of her, stood a lively and healthy Discretion and held out a bucket of magic water to her. Seeing her face, the witch fell into an indescribable rage.

"What made you so pretty?" She growled, her voice wild with anger.

"I washed with the water of wisdom," the queen said.

"You dared to disobey me," the witch cried, stamping her feet in rage.

"I will teach you. Go in your iron shoes to the ends of the world. There is a deep hole lies a bottle with the elixir of longevity. Bring it to me. I forbid you to open the bottle. If you disobey me, your spell will last forever."

Tears came to the eyes of Discretion. Seeing them, the witch laughed maliciously.

"Run faster," she hissed. "And try not to carry out my order!" The princess wandered, not even knowing which way the end of the world was. She walked many days and nights, but once her wounded and bleeding legs gave way to fatigue. She fell to the ground and thought that she was dying and only regretted that she would no longer see the green snake. Suddenly, a kind fairy appeared in front of her and said to her: "Discretion, do you know that you can only conjure a green snake if you bring the sorceress an elixir of longevity?"

"I will definitely get there," Discretion promised.

"But how do I know where the end of the world is?"

"Take this magic branch," the fairy said, "and stick it in the ground."

Thanking the fairy, the queen did everything as she ordered. With a terrible roar, the earth parted in front of her, and the queen saw a deep dark hole. And although she was very afraid, boldly went downstairs. Her courage was deservedly rewarded. Below, a beautiful young man in the world was waiting for her, and Discretion realized that it was a green snake. Seeing her, the king was speechless, struck by her beauty. For a long time, they sat, embracing, and crying with happiness. Then a witch appeared, guarding the elixir, and handed Discretion a bottle. As if to test her, the bottle was open. But Discretion remembered the lessons of fate well and overcame the temptation to drink from the bottle. The king and queen brought the elixir to the old witch. After drinking it in one sip, she became so beautiful and kind that she immediately forgot about all the nasty things that she did in life. Waving her wand, she turned the ruined kingdom of the green snake into even more beautiful than before. Then she sent the beautiful king and the wise queen home to her beloved dolls. There they lived happily ever after for many, many years.

Chapter Eighteen: Hans Bear

Many years ago, among a centuries-old pine forest, a poor coal miner lived with his wife; they recently had a baby, a healthy boy, and Hans. The boy was a real muscular guy. In infancy, he had already very surprised his parents, showing extraordinary power; once he was given three puppies to play, and he squeezed them to death. His parents scolded him for such a trick, but in his heart, they rejoiced at his incredible power and had already dreamed in advance what kind of hero they would grow up. However, they did not have much time to celebrate; now, I will tell you what happened next. In that forest, there lived a big Bear with two cubs, but once they got caught by hunters, and the Bear remained alone, the Bear could not console herself from such grief, day and night she wandered through the forest and roared with longing. The Bear saw the baby, she remembered her native children as alive, and then she wanted to take revenge on the evil people who had taken them; she rushed at little Hans to eat. But Hans was not afraid, pulled out a young tree with roots, and began to fight back bravely. The dipper marveled at his strength and courage.

"Let me," he thinks, "I will drag the little boy to my den, I will sing him with my milk, he will become strong as a Bear, and will be my breadwinner and protector instead of my teddy bears in old age." No sooner said than done; the old Bear gingerly took Hans with her front paws and, no matter how he screamed or kicked, dragged him into his thicket. Arriving at the den, she laid the foster child on the soft bed she had prepared for her dear babies, fluffed the bedding, and under her gentle grunt, Hans calmed down, tiredness exhausted him, and he fell asleep.

In the morning he opened his eyes, and the Bear is right there, sitting next to him and holding out in his claws a handful of fresh wild strawberry, which she managed to pick up early; having fed the boy, she gave him a drink of her milk; Having strengthened himself, little Hans became cheerful and began to play with the dipper, clap her hand and ruffle her curly hair, delighting his nurse. After playing with the boy, the Bear again went to the forest, but, before leaving, blocked the entrance to the lair with a huge stone, and Hans had to sit locked up until her return. Since then it has been so; in the morning, the Bear left and returned at noon; she always brought her pet a present, either a berry or a beautiful flower; after playing with the boy, she again left and wandered through the woods until evening, but, as luck would have it, I never forgot to lay a stone at the opening of the cave. Time passed, and Hans grew up and gained strength, the Bear went for him for the future; every day he was getting more and more annoyed by the big stone that blocked his path into the green forest.

Once, when the bear had crept into the thicket to get sweet honey for breakfast or to catch a fat bunny, Hans with all his strength rested his shoulder on the stone, but no matter how much he puffed up and groaned from exertion, the stone hardly moved; the Bear came back and saw that the stone was not in place; she angrily looked at Hans and the next time, before leaving, heaped more stones in front of the entrance. Hans sees there is nothing to do! He had to be patient because he still could not move the rocks, and besides, he was afraid that the Bear would not get angry if she saw for the second time that instead of gratitude for her care, he wanted to run away from her. He grew older and finally felt that now he would have the strength to scatter all the stones, and he did not want to sit locked up anymore. After waiting when the Bear left after dinner in the forest, he ran into a rock, pulled himself up... And what was his joy when the stones - Tarara! - scattered in different directions. Finally, Hans's dream came true, he got out into the wild, and God's green world opened before him, tall trees rustled around with peaks, and funny birds flooded overhead with loud trills; Hans's soul would have been joyful and comfortable if it weren't for fear that the Bear would catch him and put him in the den again.

Therefore, he started running as fast as he could and ran without looking back until he ran to the coal miner's house.

It was evening, the coal miner was already returning from the forest, he and his wife were resting, and the door was closed; then Hans banged on the door that there was urine because he had not yet passed the fear of the Bear; but then the door finally opened, the owners took pity on him and let him in; they asked Hans what he needed, and he began to beg them to take him to their workers, and told them their story, as far as he remembered.

During the conversation, the coal miner and his wife carefully examined the guest. As soon as they noticed a black mole on his shoulder, they immediately understood who had asked for their shelter and recognized their dear son, who had disappeared for so long and miraculously returned to them. That was the joy of Hans when he inadvertently found cute parents! That was the joy of father and mother when unexpectedly, a beloved son was found, at first, Hans stayed with his parents; he lived with them for a long time and repeatedly told his story to them, finally he got bored of sitting at home, and then one day he said to them:

"I want to wander around the wide world." Parents did not argue, he gathered a bag and one beautiful morning set off on the road. Having plenty of wanderings, Hans decided to take a break from wandering life. Soon he came upon a wealthy peasant estate; without thinking twice, he entered the house and asked the workers for the owner. He saw that the guy was healthy and robust and agreed. At that time, apples ripened in the garden, and the next day Hans was sent to brush off the trees.

Hans got down to business, but when he started to shake, all the branches broke and fell with the apples to the ground; the owner came to look, somehow the new worker worked, and Hans says to him in spiritual simplicity:

"Look, master, what trees are old and fragile in your garden," I shook a little, and the branches with apples hit the ground! The owner began to scold him for breaking his best apple trees, and he sent Hans out of harm's way to cut trees into the forest. The owner wanted to give Hans a good, sharp ax. But Hans did not look at the hatchet but found a thicker iron chain. He found a string and went to the forest, as he was told. And his work went: he would tie a string around a tree, tumble it down and take it for another. And so, he was already turning many trees out of the ground when the owner and his workers came to pick him up in the evening. People were surprised when they saw that he read, had knocked half of the forest, and began to ask Hans:

"Where do you, tell me, have so much strength that you can do such work in one day, with which you and ten of us a hundred days do not cope?" And Hans, for all his heroic strength, was very good-natured and flexible: seeing that people were curious to know this, he truthfully told them his whole life; then he shouldered two thick oaks and slowly took them home. And people spent a long time in the forest because they could not put down the trees fallen along with the roots on carts.

The news of this incident soon spread throughout the district, and since then, Hans was called Hans the Bear for his Bear power and for being fed by a Bear. And the owner of the estate and his workers were so terrified and so afraid of Hans' might that they only thought how to get rid of him, but no matter how hard they tried, nothing came of it. They gathered then and secretly conspired with an evil deed; they decided to squeeze Hans from the light, without waiting for when his misfortune shook. According to general advice, the owner went to Hans and said: Listen, Hans! My aunt told me in secret that her father had buried a precious treasure in my well, and now the well has dried up from the heat; crawl into the well, you look, and dig up the treasure. Hans complied with his order and climbed into the well. As soon as he went down to the bottom, the owner clicked the workers, and they began to throw stones down to lime Hans, but they did not attack him. Hans immediately knew about the evil plan. The stones did not hurt him, and he did not say anything. And they know they threw themselves and threw stones, and even when the bill went to hundreds, Hans snapped patience.

"Hey upstairs!" - Hans shouted from the well. "Run the hens away from the well so that they don't pour sand into my eyes; otherwise, I won't find your treasure forever!"

Hearing such speeches, the owner and workers were terrified; however, recovering from their fright, they dragged the millstone and threw it into the well.

"That's all, they think, now Hans won't get out."

But Hans caught the millstones with his hands, stuck his head into the hole and put it on his neck like a collar, and when they looked down to make sure he was dead, he shouted to them with a laugh:

"You didn't grant me priests that you dressed in a large priest's collar! However, it's enough to fool around, get me out of here, but alive!" And with these words, Hans launched a millstone, and it flew out so that one worker was beaten to death. And the rest were scared to death and dragged Hans out of the well. Then the owner realized that he had nowhere to compete with such a strong man, he then began to urge Hans and gave him a lot of gold: forgive, they say, Hans, for the evil intent, do not punish us, but take your little cat and go on your way. But Hans was already bored with sitting in one place for a long time; he took the gold, collected his bag, and went wherever his eyes look. He walked a day, walked another, and now people began to come across him on the road, who vied with each other in praising the beauty, the royal daughter; and they also said that the uncouth giantess was wooing her and wanted to marry her; the king, her father, was utterly embarrassed by a sort of passion-misfortune. And he promised with grief that the one who kills the giant would receive the princess and half the kingdom besides.

Hans wanted at least one peek at the princess. After all, the closer he came to the royal city, the more he heard talk about how kind and beautiful she was. Finally, he entered the city... Hans stopped in front of the royal palace and saw a princess sitting in the window, looking at the road and crying with burning tears because she was destined to become the wife of the nasty giant. Hans was so captivated by her beauty that he immediately decided to enter the battle with the giant, even though he had already destroyed three beautiful and brave knights. They dared to fight him for the beautiful princess. The first duty Hans went to the gunsmith and bought for gold received from the previous owner, a great helmet, shiny chain mail, and, most importantly, a sharp and strong sword. Dressed in armor, he appeared to the king and asked him for permission to fight the giant. The king gave Hans his blessing and promised to give his wife and half the kingdom to him besides if he emerges victorious. Hans went to battle, and the good king knelt and prayed for his soul, because he was sure that he

116

and the giant would be defeated, like his three predecessors. And Hans, meanwhile, went to challenge the giant.

Seeing Hans, the giant decided that again he could easily defeat the enemy. Therefore, he calmly leaned against a tree and chuckled at him:

"To know, and you, man, came over my head! Hurry up! See my skinny saber? Show how you lift it from the ground, and only then pull your formidable sword from its sheath."

With these words, the giant took off his massive sword from his belt and threw it to the ground. The giant thought that Hans, like the three former knights, would not be able to tear him to the heights. And with one hand, Hans grabbed a terrible sword, swung it high, and threw it so far to the side that the sword pierced the hilt into the ground. Then the giant thought:

"Looks like this hero is stronger than me, and set about persuading. I see that I doubted you in vain; you do not often meet such a fighter; let's better make peace with you; such heroes as you and me have no reason to quarrel. Do you want me to give you as much gold and precious stones as you can take in three wagons? Take it and go your way, and leave me the princess, because I love her very much and she is dearer to me than gold and all yachts in the world."

But Hans himself fell in love with the princess so much that she would become more precious to him than any gold and even her own life, and he would not exchange it for any treasures, so he did not listen to the giant, but drew his sword from the sheath; the giant also had to run after his sword and pull it out of the ground. Wow, what a jingle went when they crossed their swords, sparks, and fell from the blow! The battle did not last long; with a mighty blow, Hans blew the giant's head off his shoulders, and black blood gushed and spattered on the green grass. Hans picked up the severed head and carried it as a sign of his victory to the palace to inform the king of the good news and remind him of this promise. As soon as Hans entered the royal chambers, the king ran out to meet him and began to hug for joy. Then the king said:

"Come with me, son! I will take you to the princess and give you half the kingdom."

And so, they went to the princess, and when the king said that he had brought her a bridegroom, she, too, was glad that the giant was dead, and that she had got a handsome and handsome fellow in grooms. Hans the Bear was indeed not only a great strong man but also very good at himself.

Therefore, the princess was not without reason rejoicing when she saw her future husband, and soon handed him a hand and a heart in front of the altar. And then the old king died, and they solemnly buried him, and then Hans, who became the ruler of the whole kingdom, went with his young wife to visit his parents and take them to his palace with his brothers and sisters. They were surprised when the golden carriage pulled up and stopped in front of their wretched shack! And when they realized that the king is their son Hans, and the beautiful princess is his wife, they were so surprised and overjoyed that it was impossible to describe! But Hans put everyone in the carriage, and they, with all their retinue, went to the Bear's den to visit the adoptive mother of Hans. However, approaching the hole, they were afraid and began to ask the king to order him to turn back. But he reassured them, and when they arrived, he jumped out of the carriage and alone, without escort, went to the den. The poor Bear was lying in a layer on the bedding; she was near death.

The unfortunate thing fell ill, her strength weakened, and she could no longer, as before, earn her food in the forest; she would probably have died of starvation without waiting for Hans, but he arrived just in time. Recognizing her acceptance, the Bear got up and wanted to crawl up to him, but her strength left her, and she fell back onto her bed. Hans shouted to the servants to bring food and drink; then, he crouched next to the dipper and began to stroke and gently care for her. Ursa Major licked the king's hands with a rough tongue and looked at him kindly as if she wanted to say:

"So I waited for you, you came to render me the last service; then it's not in vain that I nourished and raised you." Little by little, the others became bolder and also went into the den, and the queen put the Bear's head on her lap, stroked it with her tender arms, and looking at her husband, also

118

tried to please the Bear in every possible way. But everything was in vain! The kind dipper was already so old and weak that she could no longer live. Throwing her last grateful look at the king, the cup stretched out and lost her spirit. And the king cried about his old nurse, and all the others also felt very sorry for her and stood over her bed for a long time. Then they buried a Bear under a centuries-old oak tree and returned to the royal city, and Hans the Bear reigned in it with his beautiful wife, and they lived peacefully and happily for many years.

Chapter Nineteen: Dragon and its Gems

Once upon a time there lived a husband and wife, lived and lived, raised a son, a boy of about fifteen. They were good people. Honest, fair, but poor. One morning, my husband went to the forest for brushwood. He walked, walked, picked out the deadwood dry, and in his heart, he prayed to God to send him a work that was more unprofitable and quieter. Suddenly, a terrible dragon crawled out from under the rock, raised himself, opened his enormous mouth, well, look at that, swallow it! The poor man saw him and measured.

"Fool," the dragon shouted, "man, I'll eat you now!" A man sobbed:

"Oh, don't eat, spare me, brother. After all, I leave the orphan son, wife. Who will take care of them!"

"Well, what a deal!" - answered the dragon. "I have to eat you, that's the whole conversation."

"Well, I'm not the first, I'm not the last!" - The person sighed. "Although I will get rid of hard work, I don't have to be in poverty and tear, to carry firewood through the mountains and valleys."

"Um... Well, since you are weak, I won't eat you, okay... Here's a gem for you. You sell it, you get rich. Come here in the mornings, bring me a bucket of milk every day, and I will give you a pebble daily."

"Well, thank you very much, brother dragon, for sparing my life and giving me a stone," the poor man replied.

They conspired, and the dragon returned to its lair. The man also picked up brushwood, but instead, home. He dumped his burden in the yard and went straight to the malls. He showed the merchant a pebble, and he paid ten lire for it. The poor man got the money and bought everything that was needed for the household; he bought all kinds of food. And the son and wife were thrilled with all of his purchases. And in the morning, he filled a bucket with milk and went to the mountains. There he called the dragon, he crawled out, drank out all the liquid and again presented a valuable stone. The man back sold his gold bit, again bought a lot of all kinds of supplies for the house. For a long time, he visited the dragon, received from him many gems, and decided to make a trip to the tomb. Before leaving his native land, he called his wife and led her to the cave, he wanted to show her the dragon and arrange with him that she would bring him milk and receive gems from him. Well, he called the dragon, he crawled out, drank all the milk, gave a pebble. Spouses parted with the dragon and set off home. My husband began to gather on a pilgrimage.

"My lord, should we marry our son before you set off?" - asked the wife.

"It would be nice, hostess," the husband answered.

"Does the guy want to get married? Call him, ask him. Kohl wants - so groom." The wife ran, clicked her son.

"Here, son, mother says that it's time for you to marry, but what do you say? I agree?" The father asked the boy.

"Since everyone is getting married, why don't I get married?" The son answered.

"Good. Well, do you have a bride in mind? Not some kind of pinwheel, but a good girl, so that we all like and come into our family like a native?"

"Yes, perhaps it is. I wanted the daughter of a neighbor."

"Well, I know her," my father replied.

"Beautiful girl. I don't know just what breed that snake is, water or maybe sand... If you don't believe, son, that all the girls are snake-breeds, get up, take a pot, scoop up water from the pond and bring it to me."

A guy came out of the house, took a bowler with him, scooped up water, and brought it to his father.

"Put your hand in the water, son, and take out whatever you catch without looking," said the father.

He dipped his hand into the water and pulled out a snake.

"You see, son, here's a snake for you. Don't be afraid, and she is watery, she won't sting. And also, it is dangerous: a snake, after all! If you meet a snake in the mountains, as if sprinkled with ashes—they call it "ashes"—run without looking back, do not try to catch how you caught a water snake. Remember, son: all women are snakes, only of different breeds. You try to find water but run away from the sand... Recognizing them is not an easy task: you need to find out everything, who is the father and who is the mother, what kind of people are grandfather, grandmother, uncle of the bride. Only in this way, you will understand what the damsel herself is."

But the son neglected bright advice and did not want to find out anything. Loved, and that's it! And true, the girl was good: beautiful, stately, tall, and white, and blush! The small one became stubborn: he would either take this one or not marry at all. Father saw that his rebellious son did not want to listen to sensible advice. Well, as the boy wished to, they did so. He became engaged to a neighbor's daughter. Well, and how the wedding was celebrated, the father went to the Holy Land. He traveled for a long time.

The older woman secretly carried milk to the dragon in the morning and sold his gems for ten lire to the merchant. Here the daughter-in-law entered the house. She noticed in an instant, cunning that the older woman was leaving the house for some time, and decided to scout (it was not for nothing that she was a snake!) To whom this mother-in-law carries a bucket of milk every day. She was furious that all the money in the hands of the mother-in-law. Why not be in her husband's pocket or even in her own hands so she can sew enough clothes for herself! Once she rose at dawn and quietly went after her mother-in-law. All spent! And the mother-in-law, returning home, as always, went to the gold mine, sold the gem, and replaced with the money. I looked at all this daughter-in-law - but instead home. She returned first so that the mother-in-law did not recognize. Here she went to bed with her husband in the evening and began to saw him: why did you get married, what kind of man are you? After all, the owner of something in the house is not you!

Your mother brings money and requires a report for each half, you only wander around the room and hands, like a fool, you breed. I need a sort of husband! Enough! Enough! And if you want me to remain your wife, so please me to obey. This morning I sniffed everything, scouted everything, I know where and why your mother goes. Tomorrow we'll go together, I'll show you everything, and as you know, kindly or dashingly, and make it so that it's not your mother, but you went to the forest with milk, and you received a profit from a gold-miner. The damned woman buzzed to her husband, all ears, and he began to envy his mother. And in the morning, he stuck to her: say yes and say where you carry a bucket of milk and how much they pay there.

"Yes, you can't answer me, son," my mother answered.

"I swore to my father. If I break the oath, I will immediately fall ill."

"Do you get sick, do not, I do not know. But you can't tell me right so that I will force it."

"Ah, son, you were not so unkind before ... Where did this come from? Maybe someone whispered something terrible to you?" For a long time, she said this, asked, prayed, but the son, trained by an evil wife, did not want to listen to anything. What to do! I had to take him to the dragon in the morning, show the gem, introduce him to the merchant who bought up precious stones.

The older woman returned home and immediately fell ill. The next morning, the mother could no longer carry milk. Seeing that the mother-in-law was sick, the daughter-in-law was delighted and ordered her husband to take the milk to the dragon himself. Well, he went to the dragon, put a bucket at the entrance to the cave. The dragon crawled out, cried out the milk, and gave the gem. The guy took the stone, and sold it, received ten lire, brought it to his wife.

"Now you look like a man, not like before!" - said the wife.

"You used to be a woman, and the man was your cursed mother."

"Yes, wife, well, now I'm a man. But you see how the mother fell ill. It's all because of me... That will die and a curse will fall on my soul."

"There will be no curse," the wicked wife answered. "And if your mother even disappeared altogether, then I would breathe freely! Do not wish her health! She lived in the world, enough, not all of her to grumble at me: either I broke a cup, then I spilled milk, then I burned my apron... He teaches, teaches that I'm such a fool, I don't know how to manage!"

The spiteful woman poisoned her husband with her speeches, she so inflamed that she would be glad to drown her mother in a spoon of water. The guy carried milk to the dragon for a long time and every day received from him a gem.

The greedy woman saw that the money was coming, well, it got into her head (admittedly, the devil made her mind), it's better not to solve the dragon and take all the gems at once than to go to it every morning for a single pebble! The guy resisted for a long time, and he did not want to kill the dragon: after all, wealth in their house brought his mercy, his gems. But the evil woman of the nobility did not know any gratitude for the good neither to the dragon, nor to her father-in-law, nor the poor mother-in-law; all tyrannized her husband to fulfill her will. Finally, the guy agreed. He made a six-armed man with an iron handle, hid it under his clothes and, as always, carried milk and put a bucket at the entrance to the cave so that the dragon would cry out. As soon as the dragon crawled out and bent over to the bucket to drink milk, the guy grabbed a stall and hit the dragon on the head. The dragon's head was as strong as iron. He waved his mighty tail hit the offender in the legs! He swayed, the guy fell to the ground, roared a good obscenity.

"Ha! Did you think of killing me?" The dragon said.

"What evil! Who taught you? Mother, does the patient lie, or maybe the wife? Well, here's the punishment for you: I'll tell you your legs now, they will numb, and you will be tormented until the pain in the crown against which you struck subsides."

The dragon encircled the guy's legs, then crawled into his dark lair. And the guy, as long as he got home, his legs became like decks. He lay down, cannot move. But the damned woman, his wife, with her husband alive! - I found another, but I didn't even want to look at the first, suffer, they say! Well, the time has passed, the father returned with the praying. Sees, it's terrible! And the wife got sick, and her son's legs are like decks. My wife told him about her illness, and the son told everything about his misfortune.

"Oh, son, you did not find a water snake; you took a sand snake as a wife!" - The father said sadly. And the next morning, he got up early and picked up a giant bucket, poured milk to the brim, and went into the forest, to the dragon. He put a bucket in front of the cave and waits for a monster not to appear. But the dragon does not come out! The older man began to call him, he asks, he prays to go out. The dragon came to the third call, greeted, told how the ungrateful guy hit him on the head with a six-man and what now bears the punishment for his betrayal.

The pilgrim listened to him and began to beg that the dragon forgive his son: the guy didn't think of such evil deeds with his mind, at the instigation of the villain of his wife, he hated his mother. For a long, long time, the pilgrim requested. The dragon finally took pity and said:

"I know, friend, that your daughter-in-law is a fierce snake. If she is alive, your whole house will go to dust. One salvation for you: your son will recover, and let her die. You force her, make her cut her little finger and let a drop of her poisonous blood fall into the patient's mouth. The poison of the serpent daughter-in-law will sort out my poison, and your son will immediately recover. If you want peace and rest in your house, do as I tell you. Now be healthy and take a pebble from me again."

The pilgrim took the donated gem and, returning home, told his son everything he heard from the dragon. He clicked on his wife and ordered her to cut the little finger. The damned woman does not agree. However, the guy was also cunning: he called her again, asked her to put a piece of some food in his mouth, and as soon as she put a hand to his mouth, bit her little finger and quickly sucked blood from the wound. Immediately he got up healthy, and the damned woman died instantly. And so, the whole family got rid of the fierce snake. Health returned to both the son and mother. The guy got married again, but first thoroughly found out about the close and distant relatives of the bride. He took the girl meek and quiet to the house, even though she was a snake, but from another snake tribe.

Chapter Twenty: To What is Written on Pody

Close your eyes and be very still, taking a big deep breath in through your nose and slowly and gently breathe out through your mouth. Take another deep breath in and slowly and gently breathe out through your mouth. One more time, big deep breath in and slowly and gently breathe out through your mouth and relax, feeling peaceful and calm. Once upon a time, the rich prince lived quietly in his castle in recent years. He had his only son, a knight, stately and strong, far famous for his courage and courage. But the old princess wanted to have a girl, so she once asked the prince to take some orphan for education. So, they did, and then they never regretted, because the girl was growing kind and obedient, to everyone's joy. Her name was Maria. Once, a messenger in dust fell into the castle and announced that the king had gone to war against the infidels and called on everyone who could hold weapons to join his army. Brave warriors stretched along the roads. The old prince, ailing and weak, sent, instead of himself, a son. A young knight went with his squad to the war, their chain mail shone like the bright sun; their swords sparkled like lightning. And in the middle of the road, a grey-haired hussar plays, sing songs, guesses each on the arm, predicts fate.

The prince's son also stopped; he wanted to know what awaited him because the war is not fun! The old man looked at his palm and said this:

"Bright prince, you have a happy share: you will distinguish yourself in the war, you will return home with glory alive and unharmed and marry a glorious girl. Only it will not be from a noble family, but a poor orphan brought up by good people. The knight threw a gold coin to the guslar, spurred his horse, and rushed off his way. The war went on for a long time; a lot of blood was shed; many soldiers were killed with bones. And as soon as it ended, the king generously rewarded the prince's son for fighting bravely, exterminated many infidels, and let him go home with glory and honors. When the prince's son rode to his father's castle, a heavy gate opened, and an old prince came out to meet him with a princess and an adopted daughter, whom they loved as their own. The young warrior jumped off his horse, kissed the hand of his father, then his mother, and did not even look at Mary. He recalled the words of the old hussar and thought: 'So far, everything that he predicted has come true. Could he have predicted that this girl would become my wife?"

Fame so turned his head so that he became proud, as is often the case with young people, he hated Mary and decided to drive her out of sight. And Maria grew up, as the songs say, a damsel-beauty, a clever-wise, transparent, meek dove. As she saw the prince's son, so handsome and so handsome, he immediately fell in love with him. And the angrier he looked at her, the more he liked it, such a girl's heart! Once, a young knight ordered his faithful servant to lower a boat into the river without oars and a rudder and put some food there. Early in the morning, he called Mary as if to walk along the shore, but the girl in a boat, and pushed her far into the middle of the river. The river flow quickly carried the ship. At first, Maria wrung her hands and cried, and then, from tiredness and grief, she forgot herself and fell asleep. At night, the boat stopped under the wheel of a water mill. In the morning, the miller pushed aside the stone, let the water run, and the motor does not spin. He went to see if some driftwood was stuck there, and suddenly, he saw a boat and, in it, a sleeping girl in a beautiful outfit. He called his wife, and the two of them moved her to the house. When Mary woke up, she told everything about her misfortune. Miller and his wife were kind people.

They took pity on the poor orphan and allowed her to live with them. Maria was a hardworking and agile girl. She began to help in the house, and soon the dusty mill sparkled like a palace. Once Maria got into a small shuttle and went to the other side into the forest for brushwood. Suddenly, the sound of a hunting horn and the sound of hooves were heard. The girl peeked out from behind the bushes and saw: the prince's son, who was hunting in these places with his entourage, was rushing towards her on a horse. The poor thing rushed to run right through the thicket. But the knight saw her and recognized her. He was angry that she again stood in his way. He hoped that she drowned or the river carried her to distant lands. He ordered his servants to catch the girl. They rushed after her, but only she, as if afraid of a doe, ran to a swampy place, and buried herself there. Servants returned in torn caftans, with scratched faces. When it began to get dark, Mary went wherever her eyes looked. She did not dare to return to the mill, and she was afraid that the prince's son would descend there. She walked, walked through the dark forest all night, and at dawn, she went out into the open field.

Far ahead, she saw the towers of a castle and went there. I reached the fence of a beautiful garden with colorful flower beds and saw, among the flowers, twelve elegant girls who embroidered on the hoop with gold and silver threads. These were the daughters of the prince here. Maria bowed low to them and asked for bread and shelter. According to her speech and expensive, albeit torn dress, the princesses recognized her as a girl from a good family who knew better days. The princess regretted the poor thing and begged her father to leave her in the castle. A day passed, another, and then one day, Maria sat down at the embroidery frame and embroidered such a lovely pattern that everyone gasped in surprise. They began to question her where she came from and what led her to them. Then Mary spoke of her misfortunes from beginning to end. Her story so upset the good princesses that they burst into tears and then hugged Mary and told her not to grieve anymore, from that day on, she would be their thirteenth sister, and they would not let anyone offend her.

They dressed Mary in expensive outfits, sat them at their table, and she became their named sister. Again, the good days came for the poor orphan. But she did not forget the prince's son, and although he inflicted so much grief on her, she still mourned for him and secretly cried. They spent many days in games and fun. And then, one day, a messenger jumped up and said that a young knight was going to them with his entourage to marry one of the princely daughters. Upon learning about this, Maria got scared and asked her girlfriends to hide her somewhere. The princes took the named sister to the highest tower of the castle and swore that not one of them would become the wife of a cruel princely son. The prince and princess received the guests with honors and said that they agreed to give the knight as a wife, the daughter who would herself want to marry him. The knight looked at the girls, everyone is good; any of them could become his good wife. He spoke kindly to the eldest, began to sigh, and boast of his wealth and glory, and she pretended to hear nothing and understand nothing, cold, like a stone. And when the prince's son started talking about marriage, she refused him. The young knight was enraged; he did not wait for a refusal. The next day, he tried his luck with his second sister, but she answered him the same. Every day the young man tried to persuade one of the daughters of the prince, but in vain.

The prince's son lived in the castle for twelve days. When the youngest sister refused to marry him, he turned green with anger, jumped on his horse, and without saying goodbye to anyone, a whirlwind flew out of the castle. And behind him, their heads bowed, stunned and ashamed matchmakers and servants stretched — how would they return home without a bride? At noon, the miserable matchmakers stopped to rest in the forest near the dilapidated chapel, where the old almost blind and deaf monk lived. And the young knight cannot find a place for himself: how to return home without a bride! After all, he promised parents to bring them a daughter-in-law! The wedding was trumpeted to all ends. To be him a laughing stock now.

"One of them will become my wife, even if I have to take her away by force!" - He decided and ordered the servants to return to the castle and kidnap one of the princesses. Servants went to fulfill the order of the young master. At dusk, they reached the castle. Just at that time, Mary went to the garden for a walk. After all, she had to sit in the tower for twelve days. Servants stole her guard, crept up to her, grabbed, gagged her so that she would not scream, and drove away.

At night they reached the chapel. And there, everything was ready for the treacherous wedding: the monk in epibranchial stood in front of the altar, illuminated by the flickering light of two small candles. Hearing the sound of hooves, the prince's son rushed out to meet his servants, grabbed the girl who had not yet had time to recover from fright, and carried her to the chapel without even looking her in the face. The monk married them in haste, as is the case in such cases, and the matchmakers with a light heart went home. The prince's son put the bride on a horse behind him and disappeared in the night darkness. In the morning, the messenger informed the old prince and princess that the newlyweds were going. According to custom, everyone went out to meet the young with bread and salt at the castle gates. They hammered into drums, and music began to play, a lot of people gathered. The wedding procession pulled up. The matchmakers were handed over to the bridegroom, who had jumped off the horse, and he nearly lost her hand when he saw whom he had brought. Mary fell at the feet of the elderly. The older adults were thrilled, and all were amazed because they had long considered her dead. They raised Mary's knees, began to hug and kiss her.

The young knight understood then that he could not escape fate. He looked more closely at the bride, and as if the veil had fallen from his eyes. Mary was more beautiful than all the beauties. He regretted that he had oppressed the orphan, threw off his arrogance, knelt before the girl, and asked for forgiveness. Maria forgave him from the bottom of her heart, for he was always dear to her and loved. They celebrated a fun wedding. Noble guests arrived from everywhere. The twelve daughters of the neighboring prince arrived and brought rich gifts to their named sister. And when the fun was over, and the guests parted, the newlyweds began to live and live in the castle of the old prince and princess. They lived to an ancient age and never once said bad words to each other. In the end, take a deep breath in through your nose and slowly and gently breathe out through your mouth. Again, deep breath in and gradually and breathe out one last time, deep breath in and slowly and gently breathe out. Whatever you are ready, wiggle your fingers, wriggle your toes, give a big stretch, and slowly and gently open your eyes. But remember, shine as bright as you can always.

Chapter Twenty-One: Chamomile

Once there was a dacha. There is still a small garden in front of her, surrounded by a painted wooden lattice. Not far from the dacha, at the very ditch, chamomile grew in the soft green grass. The sun's rays warmed and caressed her along with the luxurious flowers that bloomed in the garden in front of the dacha, and our chamomile grew by leaps and bounds. One beautiful morning she blossomed completely yellow, round like the sun; her heart was surrounded by the radiance of dazzling white small rays-petals. Chamomile did not care at all that she was such a poor, unpretentious flower, which no one sees or notices in the thick grass; no, she was pleased with everything, eagerly reached for the sun, admired it and listened to a lark singing somewhere high, high in the sky. Chamomile was so cheerful and happy as if today was Sunday, but in fact, it was only Monday; all the children sat quietly on the school benches and learned from their mentors; our chamomile also quietly sat on its stalk and learned from the bright sun and all the surrounding nature, determined to recognize the goodness of God.

Chamomile listened to the singing of the lark, and it seemed to her that in his loud, sonorous songs precisely what was hidden in her heart was sounding; Therefore, the daisy looked at the happy, fluttering songbird with a kind of particular respect, but did not envy her at all and did not feel sad that she could neither fly nor sing.

"I can see and hear everything!" She thought. "The sun caresses me, the breeze kisses! How happy I am!"

Many lush, proud flowers bloomed in the garden, and the less they smelled, the more they pushed themselves. The peonies puffed out their cheeks, they still wanted to become more roses; is it a matter of magnitude? There was no one more colorful, more elegant than tulips; they knew this very well and tried to keep as pleasant as possible to be more conspicuous. None of the proud flowers noticed the little chamomile growing somewhere by the ditch. But the chamomile often looked at them and thought:

"How smart and beautiful they are! A lovely songbird will certainly come to visit them! Thank God that I am growing so close that I will see everything; I will admire enough!" Suddenly, "queer-queer-wit!" Sounded and the lark went down, not into the garden to the peonies and tulips, but straight into the grass, to the modest chamomile!

Chamomile was completely confused with joy and simply did not know what to think, how to be! The bird jumped around the chamomile and sang:

"Oh, what a lovely soft grass! What a pretty little flower in a silver dress, with a golden heart!" The yellow heart of the chamomile shone like gold, and the dazzling white petals shone with silver. Chamomile was so happy, so glad that it cannot be said. The bird kissed her, sang a song to her, and again soared to the blue sky. A good quarter of an hour passed before the chamomile recovered from such happiness. She glanced shyly and joyfully at the lush flowers, after all, they saw what joy fell to her lot, who should appreciate it if not them! But the tulips stretched out, pouted and turned red with annoyance, and the peonies were just about to burst! It's good that they didn't know how to speak, the daisy would have gotten away from them! The unfortunate thing immediately realized that they were out of sorts, and was very upset. At this time, a girl appeared in the kindergarten with a sharp, shiny knife in her hands. She went straight to the tulips and began to cut them one by one.

Chamomile gasped. "Horrible! Now they are finished!" Having reduced the flowers, the girl left, and the chamomile was glad that it was growing in dense grass, where no one saw or noticed it.

The sun went down, rolled her petals, and fell asleep, but in her sleep, she saw a cute bird and a red sun. In the morning, the flower again straightened its petals and held them out, like a child of a hand, to the bright sun. Simultaneously, the voice of a lark was heard; the bird sang, but how sad! The unfortunate thing had fallen into a trap and was now sitting in a cage hanging by the open window. The lark sang about the vastness of the sky, the fresh greenery of the fields, and how good and free it was to fly free! The poor bird had a hard heart, she was in captivity! Chamomile, with all her heart, wanted to help the captive, but what? And the daisy forgot to think about how nice it was around, how gloriously the sun-warmed, how its silver petals glittered; the thought tormented her that she could do nothing to help the poor bird. Suddenly two boys came out of the kindergarten; one of them was carrying a knife as large and sharp as the one she used to cut tulips. The boys went straight to the daisy, who could not understand what they needed here.

"Here you can carve a beautiful piece of turf for our lark!" - Said one of the boys and, deeply running a knife into the ground, began to cut out a quadrangular piece of grass; the chamomile found itself just in the middle.

"Let's pluck the flower!" - said another boy, and the chamomile trembled with fear: if they pick it off, it will die, and she so wanted to live! Now she could get to the pitiful prisoner!

"No, it's better to stay!" Said the first of the boys. "So prettier!" And the chamomile fell into the cage of the lark. The unfortunate thing loudly complained about his bondage, tossed about, and beat against the cage's iron bars. And the weak chamomile could not speak and could not console him with a word. And how she wanted! So, the whole morning passed.

"There is no water!" The lark complained.

"They forgot to give me a drink, left, and did not leave me a sip of water! My neck is completely dry! I'm on fire and shivers! It's so stuffy here! Ah, I will die, I will no longer see the red sun, or fresh greenery, or the whole world of God!" To freshen itself up a little, the lark sank its beak deep into the fresh, cool turf, saw a daisy, nodded its head, kissed it, and said:

"And you will wither here, poor flower! You and this piece of green turf, that's what they gave me in return for the whole world! Each blade of grass should now be a green tree for me, each of your petals a fragrant flower. Alas! You just remind me of what I have lost!"

"Oh, how could I console him!" thought the chamomile, but could not move a leaf and only smelled more and more. The lark noticed this and did not touch the flower, although it plucked all the grass with thirst. So, the evening passed, and no one brought the poor bird water. Then she spread her short wings, fluttered convulsively with them, and squeaked several times plaintively: Drink! Then her head bent to one side, and her heart burst with longing and anguish. Chamomile also could no longer roll up its petals and fall asleep, as on the eve: she was utterly ill and stood there, sadly hanging her head. Only the next morning did the boys come, and, seeing the dead lark, they wept bitterly, then they dug his grave and decorated it all with flowers, and the lark itself was put in a beautiful little red box, they wanted to bury him royally! Poor bird! While she lived and sang, they forgot about her, left her to die in a cage from thirst, and now arranged a magnificent funeral for her and shed bitter tears over her grave! The chamomile turf was thrown onto the dusty road; no one even thought of the one who nevertheless loved the poor bird more than anyone else, and with all her heart wanted to comfort her.

Chapter Twenty-Two: The Dragon King

Feyr was creeping closer to the dragon egg. Every part of her body was burning. It felt like lightning was passing through her veins. The little girl smelt iron in the air, as if there was a thunderstorm brewing in between them. She could have sworn that lightning was crackling in her hair. And when Feyr stretched out her fingertips, the dragon egg shot a small bolt of electricity at her. But it didn't hurt...

"Why doesn't it hurt, Giant?" Feyr asked the talking mountain giant without looking away. The dragon egg was mesmerizing. It was pulsing and beating, like a living storm. The heart of the dragon inside was strong and full of power. It made the girl's heart race. The glow of the crystal shell glimmered in the girl's blue eyes. The lightning reflected in her gaze like two polished mirrors. Was it the dragon inside that captured the girl's attention? Or was there something deeper? A bond of some kind.

"I'm not sure, little girl. I've never seen anything like this in my life. And I've lived for over five thousand years! Maybe the Dragon Prince likes you? Or maybe there is something connecting you two? Tell me... How were you born, child? I see the lightning in your eyes."

"It's funny you mention that, sir. I was thinking about that too. On the night I was born, there was a fierce storm. Terrible and powerful. The rains howled, and the roofs were torn off the buildings. The roads were flooded and carried cars down the hill. And lightning! It was everywhere! Striking the ground wherever it could. Setting trees and houses on fire. That was the night I was born. And at the very moment I was born, midnight exactly, a giant bolt of lightning struck the ground right outside my house. Turned it right into glass. My parents told me that I was carried down from heaven by that storm and it gave me my strength of spirit and body. They call me living lightning." The girl watched the lightning flicker through the crystal of the dragon egg, smiling.

"Hm…" The giant said thoughtfully. The moss on his face and the trees on his head swayed in the wind. Curiosity danced behind the giant's glowing eyes. "I wonder…"

"What do you wonder, Giant?" Feyr asked, looking away from the dragon egg for just a moment. At that moment, the little girl could swear she heard a whisper come from inside the egg. As if the baby dragon was calling to her. She almost missed what the Mountain Giant said next.

"Well, there is a Prophecy, you see. It was created long ago by one of the wisest wizards in the land. Of course, he wasn't wise enough to know exactly who would fulfill the prophecy, but that's how these things work. The way the story goes, the Dragon Prince has very powerful magic. Dream Magic, it's called. Dream Magic has the power to make dreams come true and even grant your deepest, craziest wishes. But it also has the power to make nightmares come to life. You can imagine how that worked out. The Dragon Prince, before he ever hatched, was making the dreams and nightmares of beings all around the world come true. It was chaos. Madness! Trees were coming to life, deer were turning to solid gold, and clouds were sprouting wings. I won't even mention the

139

nightmares and monsters. Things had to be fixed. The world needed to be made right. And that couldn't be done with the Dragon Prince's Dream Magic turning the world upside down. The only solution the wise wizard could think of was to curse the Dragon Prince."

"What?! The wizard cursed this baby dragon? Why would he do that? If he was so wise, why didn't he come up with something better? And why didn't the Dragon King stop him?"

"Are you a Queen, little girl?" The giant said, furrowing his brows. They looked like two might cliffs colliding.

"What? No way. I'm just a kid."

"Then what would you know of the responsibilities a king or queen must take. It was a difficult decision, but the Dragon King wanted to protect his kingdom and the world. Not just for the citizens. He wanted his son to arrive in a kingdom he could rule. As for the wizard, magic is beyond me. The old man probably looked through countless spells and enchantments. But if an old man, older than I am, decided a sleeping curse was the best way to solve the issue, who am I to question it? And from what I know, the Dragon Queen and Dragon Queen were constantly asking the human for help."

"So they cursed the baby dragon? The Dragon Prince is cursed?"

"Yes, the Dragon Prince is cursed. But the kingdom, maybe the entire world, was saved from the wild magic. And the prophecy states that a dream from someone with a pure heart will come true and will save the Dragon Prince. Not only that, it will save the entire world. And that is why I ask how you were born. Because the Dragon Prince was also born in a storm like that. A strong, ruthless storm that tore down mountains and set fire to the fields with lightning. The Dragon Prince was also born at midnight. You two may be connected. As two bolts of lightning are still connected to the storm."

"You know... it's funny; you say that. When I look at the Dragon Prince's egg, I see something odd in it. A reflection of myself, like in a mirror. It's me, but it's not me. It's more like a feeling. And when I see the lightning strike in the egg, I feel the lightning strikes inside of me."

"What else? What else do you feel?"

"I feel a lot, but I'm also hearing something. A whisper. Almost like a song. Not in my ears, but in my head. Like the Dragon Prince is singing in my mind."

"By the Stones! This is amazing. I've seen many beings meet with this egg, hoping they would be the answer to the prophecy. None have experienced what you have. Tell me more! What is the Dragon Prince singing about, Feyr?"

"He's telling me about my dream. And how it is a good dream to chase. He's telling me about his dreams. He says we share a dream, Giant."

141

"Hohohoho! I'll be darned! Who'd have thought that a little human crawling in my earholes would have something to do with the Dragon Prince? Not me, that's for sure! No, sir. Doesn't fate work in the most wonderful ways? It's been thousands of years. Thousands have tried. And the child who comes along, wishing for nothing more than a little adventure, is the one who could save us all. What's your dream, little girl?" The giant was laughing heartily now. The gusts of wind coming from his stony lungs made the clouds below them swirl and fluff up.

"Well, it's nothing special. Honestly, it isn't. I feel like most kids have this dream. All I want is.."

"Wait! Nope! Hold that thought. Don't tell me. Tell him." And without warning, the Mountain Giant dropped the Dragon Prince's egg into Feyr's lap.

The moment the egg touched Feyr's hands, lightning began to run up and down her arms. The lightning changed color as it moved. Blue to purple to red to orange to yellow to green, all the way through every color imaginable. Feyr could feel the lightning crackling at the tips of her hair, which was starting to float up towards the sky. And then the girl started to float too. Little bolts of lightning jumped from the bottom of her feet and zapped the hands of the giant, who just laughed merrily. As lightning filled her body and made her mind race, the girl started to spin around and laugh. She'd never felt anything like this in her life. She could feel the life force of the baby dragon in the egg. She could feel the warmth and the beat of its heart. Its heart was beating at the same time as her own.

"This is amazing! I never imagined I'd get to hold a dragon egg. The Dragon Prince, no less! Not in a million years, no sir. And... am I flying?"

"We are flying, actually." The voice came from inside Feyr's head, just like before. But this time it was much clearer. It was the sweetest sound you could ever imagine. A siren's song. An angel's call. A mother's lullaby.

"Who are you?" Feyr whispered out loud.

"It's me. The Dragon Prince. The one in the egg." The voice answered told her.

"Oh yeah, duh. I guess that was a dumb question."

"No, it's fine! Don't worry about it. You're actually the first person I've ever been able to speak with even through my dreams."

"Really? The first one?"

"Yep! I've been trapped in this Dreamscape for as long as I can remember. I've heard some people call out to me from the physical realm. People asking me to make their dreams come true. Sometimes I do and sometimes I don't. But I've never been able to actually feel, see, and speak to someone from your side of the shell."

"A dream that lasts forever, huh? That must be pretty nice." Feyr wondered if the dragon wanted to wake up at all. After all, who'd want to leave their dreams behind?

"Yeah, sometimes it's great. But it's not as great as you think. In the real world, you can make your dreams a reality if you try hard enough. They can come to life, even without me. You can touch them and feel them. They're not something you made up anymore. But here in the Dreamscape, it's never like that. Dreams never become real here. They're always just dreams. And there's so much I've dreamed about that I've never gotten to experience." The dragon's beautiful voice sounded sort of sad now.

"Oh man, I'm sorry. What sort of dreams do you have, Dragon Prince?" Feyr could feel the Dragon Prince's sadness through the shell.

"My dreams? Nobody's ever asked about my dreams before. They're always asking me to make their dreams come true. You really are different." The girl could hear a bit of shock in the dragon's voice as it echoed through her mind. She hugged the Dragon Prince's egg a little closer. "I have lots of dreams. I dream of seeing my mom and dad for real. I've never seen their eyes. I dream of knowing what a real flight is like. I don't want to just imagine any more. What does fresh meat taste like? And what about the sun warming your scales? That's got to feel great!"

"I don't really have scales, but the sun does feel awesome. Don't worry, Dragon Prince. We'll get you out of there and you'll get the chance to make your dreams come true for once." Feyr pet the egg softly, before floating slowly down to the ground again. The lighting was still passing through the egg and into her body, but it was calmer now. And so was the Dragon Prince. The girl could feel it.

"I believe you. I really do." The Dragon Prince's voice was a soft whisper now. And then, after a few minutes of Feyr sitting with the egg in her lap and the giant watching this conversation with awe on his face, the voice asked her the same question. "What sort of dreams do you have, Feyr?"

"Well, it's like I was telling Mister Giant here. My dreams really aren't that special. I feel like they are dreams everyone has. You know, something every kid wants at one point."

"You'd be surprised what most people want. Go ahead, lay it on me."

"Okay, I will." Feyr sits there for a few more moments. She gathers her breath and appreciates all the magical things she has seen in just this day. "I'm pretty lucky, huh?"

"Luck has nothing to do with it, little girl." The Mountain Giant says, smiling at her with his mouth full of crystals. "You were meant to be here. You've been guided by fate."

"You really think so, Mister Giant?"

"I sure do. Nobody just happens to stumble upon a giant that's been sleeping for thousands of years. Nobody happens to just talk with a Dragon Prince trapped in his egg by a sleeping curse. Nothing happens by chance. Not stuff like this. You're lucky, sure. But you're also a believer. And I think that's why you're here."

"He's right." The Dragon Prince's voice filled the girl's head again. "There's something special about you. And that's why I want to hear your dream. So please tell me about it."

"Okay, okay. So, you know how humans and magical beings used to live together in peace? Well, I want that back. But better. I want us all to be one kingdom, one strong family together. Elves, humans, dwarves, gnomes, fairies, wizards, giants, dragons, and everything else you can imagine. I want us all to find peace together. Happiness and peace. Because I just know that everyone has something to teach someone else. And if we all learn just one thing from someone new, we could all be wise like that wizard."

Lightning flashed across the dragon egg. The giant sat there with eyes wide, looking down at the child sitting in his palms. The only sound that broke the silence was the howl of the wind against the giant's mossy head. The trees whispered to each other in the wind.

"Yes." The voice from the egg said to Feyr.

"Yes? Yes what, Dragon Prince?"

"Yes, let's make it happen. Let's make that dream come true. I've heard a lot of dumb dreams. I've made a lot of selfish dreams come true. Not this time. This time, let's have a good dream come to life."

Feyr was in shock. Could the Dragon Prince really do that? Such a little dragon? One still stuck in his crystal egg? How could he make a giant dream like that come true? But he could! Suddenly, something strange began to happen. Beautiful bolts of lightning began to swirl around the girl and the dragon prince. Bolts of light and life started to spread out along the hands of the Mountain Giant. The lightning spread further and got bright. Soon bolts were bursting and flying off in every direction. Feyr's body was warm like she was sitting next to a campfire, and she started to shake. Then, before she could ask the giant or the Dragon Prince what was happening, a bolt of lightning bright as the sun, blasts straight into the sky, sending rainbow rays of light spread out across heavens.

Everything went black. Darkness and shock made the girl faint. And when she woke up, she found a whole new world in front of her eyes. She was still laying down in the Mountain Giant's palms, but the dragon egg was gone. Also, the Mountain Giant wasn't the only giant staring at her. There was a whole ring of them! Their giant, crystal eyes were full of wonder and amazement.

"You did it, girl..." The Mountain Giant whispered. Or he tried to, at least.

Giants aren't exactly known for being soft-spoken! "You brought them back... My family. All the beings of the realms. Magical beings are everywhere!"

"That's amazing! But where is the Dragon Prince? If it worked, it's all thanks to him. He's saved the entire world. And made my dream come to life!"

Overhead, a flock of elves with bright golden wings flew about. They were singing songs in a language the girl did not know. Everything was different. Small beings that glowed. Some looked like snakes, and some looked like dragons. Others could be fish if you squinted hard enough. One bubbly critter looked like a floating jellyfish!

And then Feyr heard something. It was like the clap of thunder, but it repeated over and over. The little girl whipped her head around, but there were no clouds in sight. Where could that storm be coming from? But the child didn't have to wait long for the answer to burst through the cloud below. A massive dragon with scales of a bright blue crystal shouted out of the sea of clouds, rising high into the blue skies. Its wings crackled with lightning and its eyes shimmered a beautiful mix of colors. For a few moments, the dragon hovered overhead. The thunderclaps were coming from its wings! And then the dragon opened its mouth and the most beautiful voice came out.

"Hello again, child! Do you like my wings! I have them thanks to you!" The dragon sang out with all its heart.

"Dragon Prince!" Feyr clapped her hands, hopping up and down.

"I'm the Dragon King now, Feyr! And you are the one who gave them to me. All of this is thanks to you! You made my dreams come true. You made all of our dreams come true!" The Dragon King flapped his wings a few more times, then settled down on the Mountain Giant's hands. The Mountain Giant was smiling so bright that wrinkles were stretching across his stony skin.

Feyr ran over to the Dragon King, who lowered his head so she could hug him. "Oh, Dragon King. I'm so happy. It's all so beautiful. Like a dream! Wait. This isn't a dream, right?" The girl was scared for a moment; scared that this was all a dream.

But the Dragon King hissed softly at the girl, reassuring her. "No, child. This is real. This is all very real. What you see here is the power of a pure-hearted child's dream. Never doubt yourself or your dreams, Feyr. With them, you can make the impossible possible."

The little girl began to cry. But they were not sad tears. They were happy tears. Tears of joy and love. She was so glad that the Dragon Prince was free of his egg. She was glad that the world was once again magical. "How is everyone, Dragon King? Are they happy? Is the world at peace."

"It's better than you could ever imagine, child. The world isn't just at peace. There are no more wars. Nobody is poor or homeless. There is no more pain or suffering. Nobody gets sick here and everyone lives for hundreds of years. Even humans! It's a paradise, Feyr. Your dream, everything you hoped for, is here."

"And my family? What about them?"

"What about them, girl? They are back in the forest, the same as always. Though you might be surprised at how they've changed." The Mountain Giant told her.

"What do you mean?" The girl blinked in confusion, looking at the Mountain Giant with her bright blue eyes.

The Dragon King laughed a bit, the sound echoing through the girl's mind. It was a beautiful sound. "Climb on my back, and we'll go see them."

"Really? You'll let me fly with you?"

"Of course! I can only fly because of you, my child. Let's go." The Dragon King held out a clawed hand. Feyr climbed onto his palms and felt herself being raised up into the air. "Hold onto my claws. The breaker of the curse can't fall."

Without warning, the thunderous sound of the dragon's wings filled her ears. Feyr felt her belly roll over a bit, but that was no big deal. She barely had time to wave goodbye to the Mountain Giants and his other giant friends before they disappeared in a sea of clouds.

"I can't believe it! I'm flying. And not in an airplane or anything. I'm really flying." Feyr's heart was racing a million miles per minute. The forest stretched out below them, glowing in the morning sunlight. Magical birds were flying beside them. Their feathers were a brilliant color, like a peacock! Their tails were long and flowing like a pheasant. And their bodies were big and powerful, like an eagle!

"Fun fact, there aren't any more airplanes. People fly around on griffins and other winged creatures. Some people have a bond with dragons."

"Amazing... absolutely amazing. Oh, look, there's our camp!" Feyr pointed her finger down at the ground, where the morning campfire was flickering and whispering softly.

As they landed down on the ground, the trees bent over to make room for the Dragon King. He was careful not to crush the van or anything, but one of the tents almost blew off! At the sound of thunder crashing and the ground shaking, Mom and Dad came running out of the tents.

"What in the world is going on here?" Dad called out. He looked different. His hair was longer and woven into an elaborate braid. His clothes were more elaborate, like something out of the past.

"Feyr? Is that you? What are you doing with the Dragon King?" Mom looked different too. Her eyes were even a different color. A bright purple that almost glowed in the light. Her hair was woven into fancy braids also.

"Mom! Dad! I missed you!" Feyr said, jumping off the Dragon King's hand and hugging them both as tight as she could. "You'll never guess what I did this morning."

"Got into trouble, no doubt. Why else would you be with the Dragon King?" Dad said, laughing softly.

"Wait. You know the Dragon King, Dad?" Feyr was confused. How could her father know about the Dragon King when the dragon just hatched?

"Know him? He's our King! Everyone knows him!" Feyr's dad spoke as if the answer was obvious.

"How do you know him, little lightning?" Feyr's mother asked her.

But the little girl couldn't answer. She was still confused. How did Mom And Dad know the Dragon King? Why were their clothes different? What was going on?

"I think I can clear things up a bit. Sir. Madame. Your daughter is the breaker of the curse."

"What?!" They both gasped. Now the two adults looked shocked and confused. They looked at the Dragon King, then Feyr, then back to the Dragon King.

"Yes. She was the one who changed the world. It was her dream that was granted. It was her dream that made the world this way."

"I can't believe it..." Dad whispered softly, looking at his little girl.

Mom hugged Feyr tighter than ever, tears of joy in her eyes. "I always knew you were special, but..."

"Dragon King? I'm still confused..." Feyr said to the dragon, though the words were a little hard to hear through her mother's hug.

"It's pretty simple, Feyr. When you made your wish, the world changed. But it changed to the way things were always meant to be. The magical beings never left. I became King, and we all became one kingdom. We all became one family like you wanted. But to your Mom and Dad, it's always been this way. Nobody remembers the old world, except for you. You saved the world, my child."

Feyr still didn't understand, but that was okay. She had her Mom and Dad. But something was different. When the little girl looked up at her Mom, she noticed something.

"Mom... Your ears. They're pointy!"
"Well, of course, they're pointy, sweetheart! I'm an elf, silly. Your ears are pointy too. Don't you know that?"

When Feyr reached up to her ears, she found out that her mom was right! But that was just the beginning of the changes. The world was different now. Really different. Beautiful and magical, but everything had changed. That took Feyr a long time to get used to. For Mom and Dad, the world had always been magical. Nothing had changed for them. But the little girl still remembered the world without magic. That was okay with her. Those memories were special and helped her love this new world even more! It's what helped remind her that this wasn't all in her head. That it was really happening.

After that day, the Dragon King was always by Feyr's side. He invited her family to move into the castle with him, where they could all live together as one big family. The Dragon King taught Feyr magic and showed her all the new wonders in this world. And from then on, every day was a dream. For the Dragon King. And for the little girl who was born in a lightning storm. And they all lived happily ever after.

Chapter Twenty-Three: I Broke Grandma's Best Dish

"Grandma tell me the story of the little red basket, please," Paula begged as she tugged at her grandmother's dress.

"Paula child, you have heard that story a hundred times," her grandmother smiled down at her as she kept stirring the pudding on the stove.

"But it is my favorite, and I want to hear it again," Paula announced.

"Okay but go sit down at the table while I keep stirring the pudding, and I will tell you the story of the little red basket," her grandmother agreed.

Paula quickly climbed up onto a chair at the kitchen table and sat, waiting patiently for her grandmother to start the story.

"When I was a little girl, long, long before your father was born, my brothers and sisters and I lived on a farm out in the country with my parents. We had goats and pigs, chickens, and cows, and each of us had a couple of chores that we did every day for the animals. I was responsible for brushing the coats of the goats and for collecting the eggs from the chickens.

"Every fall, there was a fair in the nearest village, and we would take some of our animals to show at the fair, for ribbons and prizes. I had a little goat, not much more than a baby. It was the cutest little goat you had ever seen. His coat was so long that it reached down to the ground as if he was wearing a blanket upon his back, and he was not shy at all. He would go up to anyone who wanted to pet him, and I had taught him to jump up onto the stool so that I could brush him. Well, thinking about the fair, and about the goat, I started to teach him to jump through a hoop that I had made from some sturdy grapevines.

"By the time that the fair came to the village, that little goat could jump in and out of the hoop, forwards and backward, and I was sure that he was going to do well at the fair."

"And he did, he did, grandma, did he not?" Paula interrupted the story in excitement, slightly bouncing in her chair.

"He did," her grandmother agreed, continuing with the story. "A few of my brothers and sisters won either ribbons or prizes for their animals, and I won a special prize for how pretty my goat was and the fact that he could jump through the hoop that I had made for him. The judges presented me with the little red glass basket that sat on my dresser until I married your grandfather, then has sat in our dining room every day of our marriage."

"What happened to the little goat, grandma?" Paula wondered out loud.

"He grew up and became the orneriest goat that you ever did meet. He was so stubborn that he would stand out in the rain and get wet rather than going into the barn with the other goats," her grandmother replied, smiling at the memory. "Now, this pudding is finished cooking, but it needs to cool before we eat it. I want you to go play, and I will go hang the laundry out on the line, then we can have our pudding."

Paula slid down off the chair and went to the living room to get her baby doll, Dolly, her favorite toy to play with. Taking her doll with her into the bedroom where her grandmother kept a toy box, Paula opened up the chest and began pulling out toys. Down in the corner, she spotted several farm animals, including a couple of goats. Pulling the toys out, she quickly began setting up a village, stacking blocks for the houses, and making pens for the animals out of ribbon.

Humming to herself, she pretended that Dolly was her grandmother, only younger, and she was taking her goat to the fair at the village.

"And now," Paula said in her best 'man' voice, "we have the world's smartest goat here, to perform for everyone. First, he will jump up on this table, and now he will jump through this hoop, and now he will jump backwards through the hoop."

Paula danced the little goat around the fair, having him jump over and over in and out of the bracelet she was using as a hoop.

"Now, for the winners. For the best cow, you get a brick of gold," she said as she handed the cow a yellow building block.

"For the best chicken, you get a shiny purple ribbon," she announced as she tied the ribbon around the chicken.

"And for the best goat, you get a little red basket," Paula stated, getting up and running to the dining room to get the basket. Paula looked up at the basket and, even though her grandmother had told her never to play with it, she knew that she was not going to play with it, only borrow it for a little while to give to the goat. She stood up on the very tips of her toes and stretched her arms as high as she could, and, there, she could just barely reach the edge of the little red basket. Carefully pulling it towards her, she managed to get it close enough to pick it up, then she brought it down and held it with both hands.

Realizing that the goat was still waiting for his prize, Paula started running back to the bedroom, but as she ran down the hallway, her shoe caught the edge of the rug, and she tripped, dropping the little red glass basket. As she fell, Paula watched the little red basket also fall. When she landed on the floor, she heard a loud CRACK! And, looking up, she saw that the little red basket had landed on the floor right in front of her and had broken into several pieces.

Paula sat up and began to cry, knowing that she was going to get into trouble and that she had broken her grandmother's favorite dish. She sat there, crying, for several minutes, thinking about how her grandmother had told her 'No,' over and over, every time that she had asked to play with the little red basket, thinking about sitting at the dining table and staring at the little red basket and how the sunlight would shine on it and make it sparkle like a jewel, and thinking about how she was going to have to tell her grandmother that she was the one who had broken the basket.

As her tears slowed down, and stopped, Paula stood up and went over to the pieces of glass that was all that was left of the pretty little glass basket. Afraid to touch the pieces of glass, she went back to the bedroom and got the little woven basket that was in the toy box and brought it out into the hallway, then she carefully picked up each piece of the red glass basket and put them into the woven basket.

Feeling her chest hurting and beginning to cry again, Paula picked up the little woven basket and walked towards the kitchen. When she got to the doorway, she looked in and saw that her grandmother was not inside. Walking across the room to the laundry room, Paula looked inside and saw that the back door was open. Through the screen door, she could see her grandmother hanging clothes up out on the clothesline in the backyard.

Paula slowly crossed the laundry room and pushed up the screen door. Hearing the slight squeak of the screen door, her grandmother looked up with a smile but stopped smiling when she saw Paula standing there crying.

"Paula, what is the matter?" her grandmother asked as she dropped the shirt, she was holding back into the laundry basket and began walking towards her granddaughter.

"G – G – G – Grandma, I – I – I broke your little red basket!" Paula stammered as she began to cry even harder.

Her grandmother quickly took her into her arms and held her, rubbing her back and stroking her hair.

"Shh, shh, stop crying, Paula, shh, shh," her grandmother murmured to her as she kept stroking her hair and rubbing her back.

Eventually, Paula stopped crying and could tell her grandmother what had happened. How she had been playing with the little farm animals and when it came time to give each of them a reward, she was just going to borrow the little red basket, but then she had tripped on the rug in the hall, and the little glass basket had broken into several pieces, and she had put them into a real basket and brought them to her grandmother.

"I am sad that you played with the little red basket, even though I have told you many, many times that it is not a toy," her grandmother told her, cupping her face in her hands, "but I am glad that you are not hurt, and I am proud of you for coming to me right away and admitting what you had done. Now, let us go inside and get your face washed, then you can come back out here with me and help me hang up the rest of the laundry."

Paula sniffled a little as they walked back into the house, holding hands. She did not know how, but she was going to find another little red basket to give to her grandmother.

Have you ever broken something that belonged to someone else?

If so, what happened?

How did the other person feel? How did you feel?

What happened afterwards?

Do you think that Paula will ever find another little red glass basket to give to her grandmother?

If so, how do you think her grandmother will feel?

Chapter Twenty-Four: Visit a Park

After tiring days at school and long ongoing exams, it was finally a weekend approaching the summer holidays. Dino wants to visit his grandpa, but his father was going to have summer holidays after one week, and he had to wait for his father's holidays. His father promised Dino that he will surely take him to the grandpa's place. It was a weekend and Dino wanted to enjoy his holidays from the first day after the tiring days of school and long going examinations.

"I don't want to spend my first day of holiday at home. Let's make a plan with father for a fantabulous and wonderful picnic?" said Dino. "Why only picnic? We can go somewhere else. A Dolphin show, movie, playland or maybe a comic center," replied the mother. "But I want to have a picnic at a park. That would be such a great way to begin my holidays. Just imagine the quietness and scenery. I can't wait for it!" said Dino with joy. "If that is what you desire. Let me talk to your dad and convince him for the plan," said Dino's mother. Dino cheered and said, "I will come along with you to convince dad for the plan." Dino's mother nodded.

Dino's father was working on his laptop. "Father! Father! I want to go to a park for a picnic," said Dino. "Dear! I have to email this urgent assignment which may take one hour. We can go tomorrow," said Dino's father. Dino left the room silently and sat on the couch in the lounge. He was feeling sad and his heart was broken. Dino's parents didn't follow him and showed that they don't care about his feelings. Dino's eyes were filled with tears and he began sobbing.

It was all a plan. Dino's parents were teasing Dino. They silently got ready for the picnic and decided to surprise him. After thirty minutes of sobbing, Dino heard his mother talking on the phone about the picnic. Dino immediately wiped his tears and went to his mother. "Are we going to picnic?" asked Dino. Dino's dad was sitting in the corner silently and was watching the entire scene. Dino's mother started to laugh. Dino got confused and said, "Why are you laughing? I am not going to a picnic and you are making fun of me." Dino's dad said from the corner, "Son, we were just teasing you. Don't you see we have changed our clothes? Go change your clothes. Your Grandma and Grandpa will also join us." Dino's sorrow turned into happiness. He loudly cheered and hugged his parents. He ran to his room to get ready for a picnic. Dino asked his mother to prepare some sandwiches and noodles by the time he gets ready. Cranky was now full of joy as he was going for a picnic in a while.

Cranky's mother started preparing the sandwiches and noodles. "Mom, I want some nuggets and apple juice too. Grandma loves nuggets and Grandpa loves apple juice," said Dino. "It is good to think of others. I will fry some nuggets and we can purchase apple juice from the market," replied mother. Dino smiled and nodded. He gathered his toys for the picnic and closed them in a small, wooden box. He also grabbed his chopper from the closet and placed it at the back of his car. "Mother, I am bringing my chopper along. I can easily fly my chopper in that huge park," said Dino. Dino's mother nodded and continued preparing food for the picnic.

The sandwiches, noodles, and nuggets were ready. Dino's mother grabbed a wooden basket from the table and placed the eatables inside. Dino placed the basket on the table of the lounge and waited for his parents. Suddenly, Dino's dad said "Is everyone ready? Can we go for a picnic?" "I'm ready. I'm ready. let's go," replied Cranky while jumping with joy. He grabbed the basket from the table and put it in the back of the car. Dino was very excited and happy.

They all sat in a car. Dino's father gazed at the fuel gaze and said, "Oh no! Fuel is very low and we have to refuel first before going to a park." "We have to stop at a mart. I have to purchase something," said Dino's mother. "Dad! Dad! I want to have an apple juice," said Dino. Dino's dad nodded and said, "The filling stations have marts. I will refuel the car and you both purchase your stuff." Dino and his mother looked at each other and smiled. They all stopped at a lost city's fueling station. Dino's father waited in the queue for fuel. Meanwhile, Dino and his mother went to the mart. Dino purchased a bunch of chocolates, apple juice and snacks. Dino's mother purchased a sunblock and a hat. "You look so gorgeous in that hat," said Dino. Dino's mother smiled and thanked his son for the compliment. While refueling, Dino's father noticed that the tire was punctured. He looked around the station and saw a tire service shop. He parked the car near the service shop and told the in-charge to fix the tire. Dino's mother and Dino happily walked to the refueling site, but Dino's dad was not there. They looked around the station and saw that the car was parked near the tire service area. Dino's dad told them that the tire is punctured and it will take ten to twenty minutes for fixing the tire.

Dino and his mother sat on a bench, under a tree. The tree was old and huge. The shade of the tree was also very huge and it provided a comfortable environment to Dino and his family. Dino's dad kept an eye on the in-charge so that everything is done perfectly. Dino waited and waited. He ate two of his chocolates and was now feeling thirsty. He asked his mother to get him a bottle from the mart. Dino's mother informed his husband and took Dino to the mart. By the time they were out of the mart, Dino's dad had already brought the car to the mart's door. Dino was happy to see the car at the entrance of the mart. Dino and his mother sat inside the car and continued their journey to the park.

"Grandparents must be waiting," said Dino. Dino's dad increased the speed of the car and said, "I know. Sunglasses and hats got us late." Dino's dad winked at Dino and Dino started to laugh. Dino's mother smiled and said, "Tire was also my fault." The whole family started to laugh and the car was filled with joy and happiness.

The car came to a stop. Dino looked at his wristwatch and said, "It is 3 o'clock. We are half an hour late. I guess that is not an issue." Dino's dad smiled and said, "I hope so." Dino hopped out of the car and said, "Grandparents would have been tired of waiting. We must hurry." Dino grabbed the basket of toys and the basket of eatables and started walking towards the entrance of the park. "Dino, stay in our sight. Don't go anywhere without telling and be careful," said Dino's mother. Dino nodded and they all entered the park.

The park was huge with a big, colorful tree. There was a constant chirping of different birds that was as sweet as music. The park had signs that mentioned directions and instruction. Dino's dad called Grandpa and asked them for their location. Dino's dad told Dino that they are sitting at the east of the park, under a giant tree. After five minutes of walking, Dino and his family reached at the location. Dino was happy to see his grandparents. The Grandparents had already placed a reddish-white cloth on the ground. They all met each other and sat on the cloth. Grandma brought pasta and Grandpa brought pizza for the picnic. Dino cheered and told Grandma that he had brought nuggets for her and apple juice for Grandpa. Dino moved to a corner and started playing with his toys. A baby who was learning to walk, approached him seeing his toys. The baby's mother immediately ran to the baby and grabbed him. "Aww! He's so beautiful. What is his name?" asked Dino. "His name is Tom," replied the baby's mother. "I want to play with him. He is so beautiful. I would be really grateful if you let him play with me," said Dino. Baby's mother nodded and went to Dino's mother. She handed over the baby to Dino and told Dino's mother to take care of the child. "If there is any problem. I am sitting under that tree. Let me know and I will come," said Baby's mother. Dino's mother nodded and smiled.

Dino was playing with Tom. He was happy to share his toys and snacks with Tom. For some time, Tom was very happy to play with Dino, but then he started getting bored. Dino tried to make him happy, but it was a waste. Dino had no other option than to return him to his mother. Dino went to his mother and said, "The baby is tired of playing and he wants to go back to his parents." Dino's mother got up from the ground and grabbed the baby. Dino immediately ran to his snacks and grabbed his big chocolate. He gave the chocolate to the baby and said, "I hope, you remember me always." Dino's mother and Dino went to the baby's mother and handed over the child to her. Dino said, "Thank you so much. Tom is very beautiful. He loved playing with me. I wish, I can meet him again and can play with him again." Tom's mother said, "Welcome, dear. By the way, where do you live?" Dino's mother told her the address and luckily Tom's mother was their neighbor. "We never saw or heard about you," said Dino's mother. Tom's mother smiled and replied, "I am a working woman. I had to travel a lot with my child. Whenever I get some holiday, I visit this place." Dino's mother nodded and said, "Please, do visit us sometime. We would be very happy." Tom's mother nodded. Dino and his mother thanked Tom's mother for her time and came back to their picnic spot. "Dad! Grandma! Grandpa! Tom is our neighbor. They don't come here very often, as she is a working woman and travels around a lot. I am happy to have a friend near my house," said Dino. "That is very good. You should have invited them over for tea," said Dino's dad. "I wanted to, but they are leaving somewhere tonight," said Dino. Dino, his parents and his grandparents continued enjoying their picnic. They played tumbling towers, hide and seek, and chess at the park.

Dino's father looked at his wristwatch and asked everyone to wrap up as it was getting late. Dino was also very tired. He packed his toys in the basket and waited for everyone to be ready. Dino's mother cleaned the cloth and packed the remaining eatables in the basket. Grandfather gathered the garbage and threw it in the nearby dustbin. They all moved towards the parking area laughing and chit-chatting. "Why don't you stay at our place for somedays? Dino loves your presence and he would really enjoy your company in his vacations," said Dino's mother. Dino's grandparents thought for some minute and agreed. Dino cheered and said, "I have so many plans. We would never be bored, I promise." They all started to laugh and sat in the car. By the time they reached home,

Dino was asleep. Dino's father parked the car in the garage and picked Dino. He silently moved him to his bed and turned off the light of the room. Dino was tired and had slept well.

The next day, he woke up very happy. He was all fresh and energetic. He immediately cleaned himself and went to the lounge to thank his parents and grandparents for taking out time for him. Dino's parents were very happy and Dino's grandparents hugged Dino. They all sat on the table for breakfast and started eating. Dino got up from his chair and said, "I have to say, you all are the best beings alive in this lost city."

Chapter Twenty-Five: The Fisherman's Son and the Turtle

A fisherman and his wife had only one son David. They loved him so much. The boy grew up to be a handsome young man and he had learned from his father how to sail on the sea. He was the best sailor on the coast. David would sail far away from their neighborhood to places where no one around would go. His parents warned him not to go too far because he might get lost on the sea and never return home.

The fisherman and his wife were confident that their son could handle the boats well and so they never really worried about him. There were days he even returned home later than they had expected, but there was still no cause for worry. He was the only thing that mattered to them in their life and they were so proud of their son. He was the strongest and bravest boy compared to all the young boys in the neighboring coasts.

One morning, David went to fetch his net, he had set it the previous night and knew that it would have caught some fishes. When he hauled it out, he found a very small turtle and kept it in his boat. David kept the turtle in a safe place where it would be until he gets back home. The small turtle begged him, "You don't need me, and I'm too small to be eaten. Please take me back into the water. I don't want to die." David looked at the turtle in amazement. It was talking and he had never seen anything like it before. He felt for the small turtle and decided to throw it back into the sea.

Many years had gone by and David was now a grown man. On one of his journeys in the sea, he had an accident. A big whirlwind hit his boat and shred it to pieces. David was a great swimmer and managed to swim towards the land. The distance was quite far and before he could reach the land, he was already weak. The rough sea was difficult to swim through. David thought about his parents and how they would never see him again. The last thing he heard was his name and then he saw a big turtle swimming to meet him.

The turtle spoke to him, "Climb on my back and I will help you to the land." David managed to do as the turtle asked and in no time, he was sitting on the big turtle's back. The turtle told David; he was the little turtle he saved some years ago. He said, that when he too was helpless and small, David took him back to the sea. He was glad he had the chance to repay his kindness.

While the turtle kept swimming to the shore, he asked David if he wanted to know what the world looked like under the sea. David was happy to hear that he wanted to know and have the experience. The turtle hearing his excitement took David down the water. He held on to the turtle and watched as they dived deeper into the water. David could see all the gold, crystals and beautiful precious stones that were all around. The precious stones were even more when they got to a palace. The palace was very beautiful, and the beautiful scales of the fishes made it bright.

The turtle took him to the palace of the god of the sea. He told David, he was a maid to the King's daughter, the Princess. The turtle went to his Princess to let her know that he brought David to the palace. When she called him in, they both went to see the Princess. David looked at the beautiful Princess and was amazed. The Princess asked him to stay back at the palace and he readily agreed. "If you stay with me, you will remain young and handsome forever," said the Princess.

David decided to live with the Princess at the bottom of the sea. He was so happy with the Princess. He did not know how long he had spent under the sea. One day he remembered his parents and was worried that they would have been worried about his absence. Every day he kept worrying about them and was hoping to see them again. He told the Princess that he wanted to see his parents. She begged him to stay and began to cry.

"Don't go, please stay," cried the Princess, "If you go, I won't see you again."

David missed his parents and had to go so they could know he was fine. The Princess realized that nothing she said could change his mind. She decided to give him a golden box. She warned him never to open it. "If you don't open the box," said the Princess, "You will be able to find your way back." She told him that she would send the turtle to bring him back when he returned. She warned him not to forget her warning, if not, he would not be able to return to her.

David promised that he would do everything to get back to the Princess. He told her goodbye and climbed on the turtles back. He was on his way back home. For three days they were on water swimming until the turtle got to his land.

David ran to the village looking for his family. On his way, he noticed that the people there were strange. The houses had changed, and everything was not as he left it. When he got to his house, he heard the sound of music coming from the window. He knocked at the door and a stranger opened the door of his house. It was a woman. He asked about his parents, but she did not know who they were. Everyone he met to ask about his family did not know them. He found his way to the village cemetery and looked at the graves. He finally saw the names of his parents. They had died not too long he left home. When he found out the date, he realized he had been away from home for 300 years. David was so sad and found his way to the city. He thought he was dreaming. Everything had changed and he seemed as if he was in a strange land.

He remembered the Princess and looked at the gold box she had given him. He wondered if she had put a spell on it which affected the things he was seeing. He held the box up and found the lid. He quickly raised it up and a purple liquid flew out of the box. It was empty. He noticed his hands were shaking and he had grown old within a few seconds. He quickly made it to the river and looked at his reflection. He looked very old and dried up.

When he managed to return to the village, no one could recognize that he was the young person who came into the village. He struggled until he got to the seashore and called out for the turtle. The turtle did not come and then he fell down.

People rushed to meet the frail old man by the sea. David told them his story and that was the end of David. He had left the beautiful palace in the sea with the Princess to look for his parents.

Chapter Twenty-Six: Mouse of Doom

The animal keepers at the Fun-mazing Circus thought that they were so clever when they named the new baby elephant Eleanor. However, Eleanor the Elephant is a mouthful and they have regretted it evermore.

Eleanor (Ellen for short) was the most adorable baby animal that the performers had ever seen. She was the color of clouds before a storm and tripped over her own ears more than anyone has ever tripped over anything. She was a bubbly little creature and would never shy away from learning new tricks. Ellen wore a periwinkle bow around her neck because she had always loved the color. A few of the trainers lamented that she was the sassiest little elephant and deserved her own hour in the show to perform her tricks. Ellen loved her job in the circus and had a natural presence on the stage. She was also a huge draw for the crowds, and they used her image on all the printed advertisements. Ellen had learned a new trick where she would lay down behind a large board that served as a wall to block her body. One of the trainers would play snake-charming music, and she would allow her trunk to slowly dance up above the wooden wall. The audience would think that she was a snake. She and the trainer would keep this illusion going for quite a while before she would stand up and reveal herself to the audience. They would scream and applaud her so loudly. She would stumble off the main stage, accidentally stepping on her ears once, or three times.

Ellen was a wonderful performer and loved her life with her circus family. One fateful day, the trainers told her that she needed to work on her grace and balance. She was understandably upset. Ellen was a star! The audience seemed to love her exactly as she was, so why were they asking her to do something that was in opposition to her nature? It wasn't like they were asking her to do a new trick, they were asking her to change her nature. This brought Ellen to the point of tears and she felt as though they were telling her that she wasn't good enough. She didn't take the revelation well and ran to her specialized enclosure to sulk. The peppy pink and purple colors that adorned her walls were not enough to lift her spirits at this moment, as they had been in the past. She buried her head in a pillow and enclosed her ears around her, in a further effort to drown out the world around her.

Ellen sobbed for a while, knowing that it is important to allow oneself to express one's emotions. As she began to calm down, she noticed a rustling in the stillness of her room. A tiny noise penetrated the quiet and caused the small elephant to take pause. She slowly pulled her ears from over her eyes to find the culprit. The movement stopped and Ellen decided that it must have just been the wind playing tricks on her very sensitive hearing. All the tears had worn our young hero completely out, so she repositioned her ears and readied herself for a nap. No sooner than she had covered her eyes again, that darn noise came back. She was determined to find the source, so she moved slowly and methodically this time. Ellen allowed her ears to gently fall away from her face, as though she were asleep. The tiny disturbance paused for a moment and then continued, probably safe in the knowledge that the elephant was resting. That is when she saw the creature responsible for the ruckus and her heart sank. It is at this point in our story that we must take a moment to understand a crucial fact about elephants. They have a natural aversion to small animals. This is a widely accepted fact, but we must understand why. In the chaos of excitement, it would be very easy for a tiny creature to misplace its' sense of direction and run right up an elephant's trunk. It is speculated that elephants are born with this disdain for smallness, and object to a tiny thing in the same way that you or I might object to a snake or a spider.

A small brown mouse stood anxiously in the corner of the room, looking for leftover straw for her own house. This tiny mouse had a nerve of steel and was mostly unbothered by the elephant, while trying to be very mindful of its' awareness. She was a scavenger of other's junk, but was also very careful not to take anything of sentimental value to anyone else. The tiny mouse occasionally glanced up at Ellen, and finally realized that she was being watched. They both let out a terrible shriek and the mouse scurried away in a blind panic. Ellen was still frozen with fear and concerned that the mouse might return to finish what it started. She stayed glued to her pillow for some time before she gathered her courage and went to find her trainer. The trainers searched her room from top to bottom and found no evidence that a mouse was ever there. They assumed that the small elephant was still upset about their earlier request to learn balance and was allowing that to cloud her perception. They informed Ellen that everything was quite alright and then left her again, to her own devices. What a terrible day for our elephant. Later that night, there was a tiny knock at the bottom of the entrance to her room. Ellen told the knocker to come in, half asleep, out of habit. The tiny brown mouse stood to wait in the doorway.

"I am so sorry that I gave you such a fright earlier. It was wrong of me to be in your room without permission. I was looking for straw for my own house. I really did not mean to frighten you. My name is Ida." The mouse said.

"Take anything you want, except for my bow!" Ellen screamed back. She was visibly shaken by the mouse's presence, and willing to do anything to rid herself of this tiny monster.

"Tell me Elephant, why are you so terrified of me?" The mouse asked.

Ellen explained that she was compulsively worried that something as tiny as this crafty little mouse might run right up her trunk. This seemed to be a fear that all elephants possessed, and she was surely not alone in this belief. Ida shook her head in dismay, knowing that there is no way that this elephant has ever had an experience even remotely like the one that she has been envisioning. This sort of thinking led to a lot of negative mouse stereotypes. Even if Ida had a habit of breaking into rooms and stealing trash, she'd never even think of clogging up someone else's nose tube thing (mice aren't hyperaware of elephant body parts). She did her best to explain to the elephant that she was actually a huge fan of her performance and had often wondered what it would be like to be on stage herself. Ellen found herself feeling more and more comfortable with the mouse as their conversation went on. She even confided in Ida about the trainers, and their request that she should overcome her natural

172

clumsiness. Ellen then talked at length about how she knew that she could never be as graceful as some of the other animals. Ida had always been a good listener. She took the time to really understand Ellen's hesitation with the request, before finally offering her advice:

"Please don't think of it as the trainers are asking you to change a part of your personality. They're asking you to evolve into a better performer. You aren't going to be a baby forever, and someday you will need to know how to get around without hurting yourself. Becoming better is never a bad thing and if you think that you can't do it… well, you are just wrong. You need to change your thought process around change; change is a wonderful thing. Change is how you become the person that you're meant to be. Instead of tearing yourself down, you should build yourself up. Practice your heart and know that you can overcome this obstacle just like every obstacle." The mouse said.

Ellen was quiet for a moment while she considered Ida's words. She hadn't even considered that they were preparing her for the future. She thought that the trainers wanted her to change as an attack on her talent as a performer. She agreed to try her best to become more graceful and she asked her new friend to help her train. The next day the two set out to teach Ellen balance and awareness of her surroundings. Ida sat atop her head and pointed out every unlevel piece of ground as they traversed a field behind the circus. Ellen was unsteady on the first day of practice and became more and more frustrated as the day went on. She stumbled over her ears swayed from one side to the other. Ellen sighed and sat on the edge of the field, upset with herself for failing. Ida, still clinging to the top of the small elephant's head, was having none of this. She explained that failure is a necessary step in the process of mastering a skill.

"My first house was a wreck, easily found and destroyed by larger animals. The next time I built a house, I did so in a more secluded environment. Every time I rebuild, my houses get better and better. This is not defeat; it's only your first step in the process." The mouse explained.

The next day, the pair returned to the field. They tied Ellen's ears back with her favorite bow and there was an instant change. The little elephant was able to see all around herself now and no longer had to worry about tripping over every rock they crossed. Ida realized that this whole time, her ears had been the issue. The two of them still practiced all day, but the difference in Ellen's stride was remarkable. From that week on, the two were inseparable. Ida rebuilt her house in Ellen's room and two stayed up laughing late into the night, every night. If Ellen had let her fear get the better of her, to this day she would be a clumsy elephant with no best friend.

Soon Ellen had convinced the trainers to let Ida try out for the circus too. She was such a talented little mouse, that the circus was eager to have her. Ida and Ellen became known worldwide as 'The Unlikely Duo,' and eventually, they performed all of their acts together. Ellen insisted that Ida take one of her favorite pink bows to that they could match on stage. Ida was especially nimble and excellent at acrobatic tricks, though ensuring that the audience could see her was not always the simplest task. One of the more industrious trainers actually invented a huge magnifying glass that became a staple in their acts. The trainers would roll out the enormous contraption and the crowd would go wild. Watching in eager anticipation as the mouse flipped around Ellen, who was always very careful to gently catch Ida with her trunk.

Then Ellen would dance around the ring as though rhythm and grace were gifts, she was given at birth. She would sashay around throwing out one foot at a time. The audience loved her, and her best friend Ida, and they continued to be a favorite attraction for many years to come. The most treasured of their shows involved Ida pretending to scare Ellen, who would then run through a very difficult obstacle course that consisted of many challenging jumps and twists. In a playful spirit, they named this act 'The Mouse of Doom.'

CPSIA information can be obtained
at www.ICGtesting.com
Printed in the USA
BVHW090321040521
606332BV00006B/1385